# IN THE BIN

## Reckless & Rude Stories
### from the
## Penalty Boxes
### of the
# NHL

### by NHL Official
# LLOYD FREEBERG

Triumph Books
Chicago

## To Anastacia, Jennifer, and Logan
## . . . beyond MVPs.

Printed in the United States of America

This book is available in quantity at special discounts for your group or organization. For more information, contact:

Triumph Books
601 South LaSalle Street
Suite 500
Chicago, IL 60605
(312) 939-3330 Fax (312) 663-3557

Book design by Patricia Frey
Cover design by Salvatore Concialdi

ISBN 1-57243-232-2

Library of Congress Cataloging-in-Publication Data

Freeberg, Lloyd, 1941-
       In the Bin: Reckless & Rude Stories from the Penalty Boxes of the NHL /
Lloyd Freeberg.
          p.      cm.
     Includes index.
     ISBN 1-57243-232-2
     1. National Hockey League–Humor. 2. Hockey players–United States–Humor.
3. Hockey Players–Canada–Humor. 4. Freeberg, Lloyd, 1941-      . I. Title.
GV847.8.N3F74  1998
796.962'64'0973–dc21
                                                                98-39824
                                                                   CIP

# Contents

# Section Four: Stranger Than Fiction ............129

# Index ...............................................213

# Introduction

Without a doubt, I've not only played in more Stanley Cup finals than anyone on earth, but I've scored the winning goal in most of the games, usually in overtime off a feed from my older brother, Roger. Never heard of us? That's probably because these finals were played in our backyard rink on Jefferson Avenue in St. Paul. Not quite the same as the ice on St. Catherine Street in Montreal or on Madison Street in the Windy City, but when you're ten years old, the differences aren't all that important. What is important is that you're playing the greatest game on earth, dreaming about scoring the big goal at crunch time, and hoping someday to make it all the way to the National Hockey League.

By the time I was in high school, I had been fortunate enough to play on a national championship junior team and to have competed in international tournaments, experiences which drove home the point that unless there should suddenly be a big demand for small players with marginal, nay, questionable, skills, my dream of playing at that level could more appropriately be classified as an hallucination. Well, at the tender age of fifty, I finally did make it to the NHL, although not quite the way I had hoped I would.

Hired in 1993 as an Off-Ice Official by the National Hockey League, I have been assigned continuously to the Arrowhead Pond, home of the Mighty Ducks of Anaheim, with occasional travels to other arenas during the playoffs. During this time, I have worked both the home and visitor penalty boxes, run the scoreboard clock, kept the game stats, sat as a goal judge, and even spent one game in the video goal booth. This book is a compilation of those experiences and up-close observations of what really is the "coolest game on earth." I hope that when the last page is turned, the reader has not only been entertained, but has gained a unique insight and respect for those who play, coach, officiate, and organize the most demanding team sport of all.

If this endeavor is successful, it is due to the contributions of many people. First and foremost, to Wendy Lindley, my deepest appreciation for your unfailing support and encouragement. To Shelly Castellano, Henry DiRocco, Anastacia Freeberg, Tony Guanci, Bill Gurney, Luise Healy, Rick Hutchinson, Doug Jones, Matt Lindley, Robert Masello, Mark O'Neill, Dave Pace, Baron Parker, Gary Pence, Marc Posner, Rob Schick, and Jim Stevens, my sincere thanks to each of you for your unique and essential help.

In particular, I owe a considerable debt of gratitude to the staff of Triumph Books beginning with Mitch Rogatz, whose enthusiasm was infectious, and to my editors, initially Siobhan Drummond, and to completion, Laura Moeller, who made this project a reality. Also, and importantly, to Sarah Burgundy and Chris Smith, whose behind the scenes work was needed and greatly appreciated.

I would also like to thank my fellow Off-Ice Officials Steve Bashe, Serge Gange, Gary Gerwig, Doug Ingraham, Greg Jowk, Ed Middleton, Dennis Milligan, Rick Nichols, Dave Pace, Mike Pons, Fred Schwanbeck, Dennis Thurston, Chris Valois, Tom Wardell, and Peter Zeughauser. To my NHL colleague, Bill Bedsworth, my special thanks, not only for his advice, but also for recommending me for the Off-Ice Official job in the first place.

Lastly, to the countless number of hockey fans with whom I've had the pleasure of playing, talking, or watching hockey, enjoy . . . this is for you.

Lloyd Freeberg

San Juan Capistrano, California

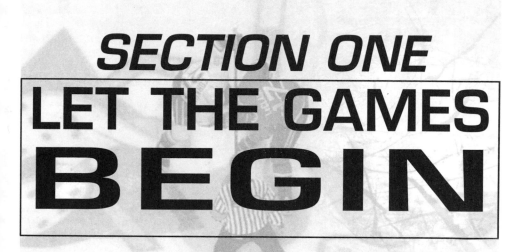

# SECTION ONE
# LET THE GAMES
# BEGIN

# Before Play

## First Hollywood, then the NHL

On December 9, 1992, the National Hockey League granted conditional approval for a franchise to be established in Orange County, California, by the Walt Disney Company. On March 1, 1993, it was announced that the Mighty Ducks of Anaheim would begin play in the 1993–94 season. But before the first puck could be dropped, a staggering amount of organizational work had to be done in record time. To accomplish this, Disney forged a management team of professionals whose charter was not only to get the team up and skating, but to present a quality, entertaining sports package for fans both new and experienced.

Disney Chairman Michael Eisner sought an executive to lead this effort who had management principles similar to his own: set high standards, make a total commitment, lead by example. Tony Tavares was a natural choice to be the President of the newly formed Disney Sports Enterprises (DSE). His training as an accountant, his knowledge of the sports industry, and his proven management skills developed while CEO of Spectator (a major facilities management company) would be absolutely essential to any successful venture of this magnitude. What Tavares also brought to the table was a personal dedication to success that permeated the entire project. And beginning June 7, 1993, Tavares would need every bit of that dedication.

On that day, a press conference was held to confirm the new name of the team to be the Mighty Ducks of Anaheim and to unveil the team logo and team colors of purple, jade, silver, and white. The announcement was greeted by a resounding groan from hockey purists, who had already reacted unfavorably to the team name, and were now certain this new look would never fly. Complaining the colors and logo were demeaning to the macho image of hockey, some predicted players would refuse to be dressed up in outfits that looked more like movie costumes than sports uniforms.

Before the first game had even been played, the Ducks had become the laughingstock of the league and material for standup routines every-where. Forgetting that another National Hockey League team named after a bird (and one that couldn't fly, at that) had its name on the Stanley Cup, critics predicted certain failure. They apparently also forgot who was doing the marketing. The imagineers who endeared mice and mermaids to the world set about doing the same thing with puck-passing ducks.

When the doors to what became known as the Arrowhead Pond of Anaheim opened on October 8, 1993, for the first National Hockey League game in Mighty Ducks history, it was clear that Disney's marketing talent had risen to the task. Not only were all 17,174 seats filled with cheering fans, but most of them were wearing the once-ridiculed team colors. In fact, Mighty Ducks merchandise had quickly surged to number one in worldwide sales of such items, leaving the previous sales-leading San Jose Sharks in its wake. The press box and press lounge were filled beyond capacity. Working members of the media were far outnumbered by Disney guests and staff, local community leaders and politicos, and National Hockey League Officials. Wearing the official NHL blazer and tie, I was still amazed that I was one of them.

*Where it all begins: face-off at the Arrowhead Pond.*

> The imagineers who endeared mice and mermaids to the world set about doing the same thing with puck-passing ducks.

My credentials for being an Off-Ice Official were somewhat sparse. Certainly, hockey was a tradition in my family growing up in Minnesota. My grandfather and father had each played on state senior championship teams, and I had been a member of a national championship junior team. However, I had only officiated one hockey game ever, which was way less than successful. When a referee failed to show up at a Pee Wee game, I was reluctantly pressed into service. Being in high school at the time, and just slightly older than the players, I decided to call only the most obvious penalties. Unfortunately, by the time I had the nerve to call a penalty, someone else needed to call the Red Cross. As I whistled a player for a blatant trip, his father, who looked big enough to pick up a cement truck, yelled, "I'm gonna come out there and show you what a real trip is like." Sometime during the melee that followed, I became a staunch advocate for arming officials.

Remembering this incident as if it happened yesterday (rather than 35 years ago), I hesitantly applied for a position as an Off-Ice Official assigned to the Mighty Ducks venue. The Off-Ice Officials crew consists of a supervisor, an assistant supervisor, an official scorer, a video goal judge, two goal judges, a penalty timekeeper, a penalty box attendant, and two statisticians. The responsibility for selecting the crew was given to Tony Guanci, who was designated by the league as crew supervisor. Together with assistant crew supervisor Steve Bashe, Tony conducted the screening and interviewing of nearly 90 applicants. I began to feel more comfortable when Tony and Steve explained the duties of the penalty box attendant: open and close a door; count backwards out loud from five; hand the linesman replacement pucks. Hey, no problem I thought. As long as some big guy doesn't threaten to demonstrate the penalties on me, this would be a walk in the park. What could be simpler?

"Oh, and there will be rubber gloves and a medical waste bag with you in the penalty box for the bloodied items."

Reality came back in a heartbeat, and with it came the image of the penalty box people at the Spectrum in Philadelphia . . . wearing helmets. Helmets? Is this job safe? Is it possible I would be one of the bloodied items Tony was referring to?

A friend of mine has a collection of hockey fights . . . 3,500 hockey fights . . . and if you watch them for any length of time, it becomes immediately apparent that hockey fights are the real deal. Here are two strong, fit, professional athletes trying to knock each other into next week, and then are eventually shoved into the penalty box where they continue to create all kinds of havoc. I began to realize I wouldn't simply be the host, I'd be the warden. While everyone else would be watching the game with friends or loved ones, I'd be locked in a box with raging bulls. Forget a helmet. I'm thinking body armor and an automatic.

"Well, Lloyd, do you want to be a member of our Off-Ice Officials crew?"

How could I? I'm sure my health insurance policy has this paragraph under coverage exemptions entitled "hazardous activities." And I'm not getting any younger. I knew what the right answer was, but before I could say no, I said yes. Whatever the potential hazards, there was no way I was going to miss being this close to the game I've loved since I was a little kid skating on our backyard rink. A total of ten individuals were selected for the crew with final approval coming from the National Hockey League Supervisor of Officials. A diverse group consisting of pilots, entrepreneurs, computer experts, lawyers, even an Appellate Court Justice, we all shared a common characteristic: an intense passion for the "coolest game on earth."

As Opening Night approached, we all felt an unparalleled excitement at not only officiating our first National Hockey League game, but also the first game in the history of the Mighty Ducks of Anaheim. Adding to the excitement was the fact that the Ducks' first opponent would be the Detroit Red Wings—one of the original six teams, and possibly the strongest team in the league. But while most prepared for a thrilling offensive show by the likes of Fedorov, Coffey, and Yzerman, I was aware that chances were good I would be spending considerable time with hockey's bad boy, Bob Probert. The uppermost question in my mind was not who would win the game, but rather: would I survive it?

# Opening Night Glitters

## Fireworks, Dancers, and a Giant Duck

Opening Night came amidst great expectations. This was Disney, after all, and rumor had it they had spent more on the opening night show than on any one Mighty Ducks player. Walking onto the ice heading to the penalty box, I couldn't help being overwhelmed with excitement. This was only the seventh time in the history of the National Hockey League that expansion had occurred, and if anyone could make it a success, Disney could.

But to do so, this multibillion dollar media and entertainment giant would have to apply all of its considerable talent and resources. For one thing, just a few miles up the Interstate was the home of the Los Angeles Kings—so close, in fact, that Disney had to pay them an indemnity for infringing on their turf. This raised the question of whether the Mighty Ducks could compete with them for what was thought to be a limited fan base. The Kings, in the National Hockey League since 1967, now had solid fan support, a talented and popular team that had just come within a curved stick blade of the Stanley Cup, and Wayne Gretzky, the number one marquee player in the universe.

Looking around the arena, I found myself comparing it with the Great Western Forum, where I had trekked with my son for several years as a

Kings season ticket holder. Once referred to as the "Fabulous Forum," it had been built in 1966 and was definitely showing its age. Situated in neither a convenient nor desirable area, lacking revenue-generating luxury suites, and having limited seating all spelled impending doom. By contrast, the Arrowhead Pond of Anaheim was a brand new, state-of-the-art facility more closely resembling a large estate than a public arena. Using over 250,000 square feet of marble on the interior, it accommodates 17,174 hockey fans in theater-style seating or in one of the 82 amenity-laden luxury boxes. And on this night, there wasn't an empty seat in the house.

As I got to the penalty box, the referee and linesmen skated onto the ice, bringing an uncharacteristic cheer from the fans. As the house lights began to dim signaling the much anticipated debut of the Mighty Ducks of Anaheim, the officials joined me in the box for a ringside view of the opening night festivities. Fittingly, the first game would be officiated by Ron Hoggarth, a senior National Hockey League referee who, until that night, thought he had seen everything. As he sat back for the show I wondered how he would react to Disney's marketing of the game he loved. I wouldn't have long to wait before I found out.

First came the ice dancers twirling and spinning onto the ice wearing brightly colored tutus, leotards, and scarves. Then came the female ice dancers to join them. Despite the music and the noise from the crowd, I thought I could actually hear Hoaggy's eyes rolling back in his head. Pointing at one of the ice dancers, I turned to him and said,

"Amazing, isn't it? Bob Probert dancin' around out there like that just to pick up a lousy hundred bucks."

Having already seen the bizarre, his eyes widened as if maybe it really was Probie in the chiffon, but he quickly realized not even the Walt Disney Company had enough money to make Probert do that.

We all jumped in unison when fireworks, cleverly hidden near us,

*The ill-fated Iceman was part of the Ducks' Opening Night extravaganza—a ceremony only Disney could have pulled off.*

went off in a series of loud explosions. Smoke and artificial fog filled the arena as the music tempo and volume increased to ear-splitting levels. Suddenly, out of the Zamboni entrance roared an off-road quad ridden by a crazed figure dressed in a rhinestone body suit and waving an electric guitar that was emitting a deafening sound not unlike that of a chain saw. This was the "Iceman" Disney had spent six months auditioning. Looking for a person who was an accomplished musician and skater, they found many who could do one or the other, but not both. We pretty much figured out this guy was not a skater when he began running around the ice in sneakers. But as we found out later, he apparently was a better skater than musician.

The Iceman was soon joined by the team mascot, a giant, all-white duck who skated around the ice in imitation hockey gear, alternately entertaining and terrorizing fans by hurling himself on the glass at great speed. By now, I was hoping there were smelling salts somewhere in the penalty box for Hoggarth, who was groaning out loud at each new spectacle on the ice.

From the Zamboni entrance, nearly one hundred kids involved in local youth hockey programs skated in a serpentine pattern onto the ice, and stopped to form a funnel through which the players would be introduced. I strained to see my son, Logan, who was part of the program, but the fog bank seemed to be settling in for the night.

One by one, the Mighty Ducks of Anaheim were introduced as they skated through fog thick enough to stop traffic, many of them looking sheepish as they peered out of the haze towards their cheering, but as yet indistinguishable fans. I leaned over to Hoggarth and said,

"I wonder what the old-time fans in Canada would do if they saw this show?" His only comment was a loud snort. Soon enough the pregame show was over, and the Detroit Red Wings show began.

Midway through the game, with great fanfare, the Iceman was reintroduced, this time as he stood in the stands. The spotlight came on him, and he began furiously banging on his guitar and singing. Alas, due to

> And on this night, there wasn't an empty seat in the house.

technical difficulties, not a sound could be heard. The crowd, moments before boisterous, was now eerily silent as everyone strained to hear, but to no avail. There he stood, as if in a silent movie, gesturing wildly, the only sound to be heard a rising, then deafening chorus of boos. The spotlight was turned off, and as quickly as the Iceman had cometh, he wenteth, never to be seen again. Many months later, as I made my way to the Video Goal Judge's area high over the arena, I spotted his guitar partially hidden up in the catwalks. For all we know, he may still be up there, silently crying for help.

As the game progressed Detroit made known its intention to spoil the Mighty Ducks' debut with a barrage of goals. But as the referee blew his whistle and signaled a Detroit penalty, I knew my own show was about to begin.

# My Near Death Experience

## "Buddy-buddy" with Bob Probert

Not surprisingly, my first official guest in the penalty box was Bob Probert, then of the Detroit Red Wings. Reigning heavyweight champion of the National Hockey League, Probert had fought and beaten every pretender to his throne since joining the league in 1985–86. As he skated towards the visitor's penalty box, I could see why he won a whole lot more than he lost. Though imposing enough at 6' 3" and 225 pounds, it was the look on his face that was pure intimidation: a scowl punctuated by scar tissue that would cause those who cross his path to immediately begin handing over their wallets. Then known, along with tough Joey Kocur, as one of Detroit's "Bruise Brothers," Probert's reputation as a brawler simply could not be exaggerated. Being roughly the size of his shin pads, I started to think that retirement on my first night was better than being confined in a 5' by 14' area alone with Bob Probert.

It was late in the game when Probert picked up a fighting major for using an opponent as a speed bag. We were soon joined by his teammate Ray Sheppard, who was assessed a minor penalty with just three minutes left in the game. As I stood at the other end of the bench monitoring the penalty clock, I soon became aware of the two of them arguing. "You take

> Frozen by Probert's glare, I awkwardly stood there wondering if I could jump into the scorer's booth.

them, it was your idea," Sheppard was saying. "I don't have any place to put them. You take them," Probert would counter. And on it went, back and forth. Curiosity getting the better of me, I looked over to see what the reason for this bickering was, and discovered that Probert was holding six of the opening night commemorative game pucks he had removed from the ice bucket. He was trying to find a way to sneak the pucks from the penalty box to the players' bench on the other side of the rink, and Sheppard was being of little help. "I can't take them. I've got to go back on the ice before you. Just stick them in your gloves." But Probert kept insisting: "They won't all fit, man, and I've got no other place to put them."

For a reason I will likely never be able to explain or understand, I suddenly blurted out, "Hey, Probie, why don't you just shove them down your pants?" No sooner had these words been spoken when Probert turned to me with a look on his face that was a frightening mixture of surprise and anger. This was the same look I'm sure many of his sparing partners had seen right before the gloves came off and the lights went out.

Frozen by Probert's glare, I awkwardly stood there wondering if I could jump into the scorer's booth quickly enough to escape what was surely coming. Just as I thought I was about to become the first Off-Ice Official mauled in the line of duty, a strange thing happened. Sheppard began to laugh, an infectious laugh that continued until, to my immeasurable relief, Probert began laughing as well. Thankfully, the penalties expired and both players, still chuckling, left the box to rejoin the game,

## PENALTY BOX

**Bob Probert**
Games Played: 727
Total Points: 373
**Penalty Minutes:** 2,975

*"Was it something I said?"* The author couldn't figure out why his friendly suggestion made Bob Probert so angry.

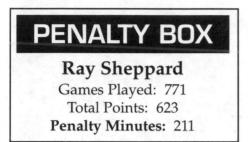

## PENALTY BOX

### Ray Sheppard
Games Played: 771
Total Points: 623
**Penalty Minutes:** 211

Sheppard with a big grin, and Probert with his rubber treasure trove.

The next day, I awoke replaying in my mind the previous night's excitement. The opening night glitz, fireworks and all. The Iceman's coming and quickly going. The giant duck mascot and the skating cheerleaders. But continually intruding into my reverie was Probert's hidden puck trick. Why had he given me the fierce face? Geez, couldn't he take a little joke? Was this guy so sensitive that suggesting he shove the pucks down his pants would cause him to freak out?

An icy chill began to pass over me as the mental fog started to lift, exposing a newspaper story I had read sometime before, but was only now recalling: Probert had been suspended from playing in the National Hockey League for one year after being caught smuggling cocaine into the U.S. from Canada. And he had concealed it by . . . gasp . . . shoving it down his pants.

It has been reported by those who claim to have had a near death experience that a great white light preceded the actual act of dying, and that the death was interrupted by some event which allowed the subject to live to tell about it. Well, my near death experience came shrouded all in red with a big number 24 on it. And I am fully convinced that had Sheppard not begun to laugh I would literally have taken this story to my grave. So you can talk about your Gretzkys, your Lemieuxs, and your Messiers. But in my book, Ray Sheppard will always be the Most Valuable Player in the NHL.

# Duck Tales

## If You Think Pro Hockey Is Tough, Try Being the Mascot

No other organization in the world is more qualified to create a mascot than the Walt Disney Company. Getting humans to adore animals they would otherwise be trapping is a task Disney has been performing expertly for decades. And so it was with great anticipation that fans awaited the opening night debut of the Mighty Ducks of Anaheim mascot.

The Mighty Ducks logo had already been unveiled to a mixed review, most feeling it was decidedly cartoonish, but still evoking the rough, tough image of professional ice hockey. Whether the mascot wearing it would be more hokey than hockey would be determined during its inaugural game introduction on October 8, 1993.

The moment the giant duck glided onto the ice the resounding applause signaled yet another success for the imagineers at Disney. Wearing a Mighty Duck jersey, simulated goalie pads, and the trademark scowling duck bill, he romped his way into the hearts of fans both young and old. As the result of a fan Name-the-Mascot contest, the giant duck became known as "Wild Wing," a name it would live up to in ways no one would have predicted. Whether entering the rink from the rafters by guide wires, rappelling down from the roof, or driving onto the ice in an off-road vehicle, his antics provided as much (and on some unfortunate nights, more) entertainment than the sub-.500 team did.

But it hasn't always been a bed of feathers for he of the menacing bill. Luckily, this duck has more lives than a cat, having survived several harrowing experiences that would have had lesser fowl winging their way south permanently.

First was the hanging incident. With dramatic music to herald his entrance, Wild Wing customarily begins the pregame show being lowered by cables from a roost in the rafters down to the ice surface some 100 feet below. Usually, this stunt goes off without a hitch, much to the delight of the fans. Unfortunately on this occasion, as he was being lowered, dancing in air to the accompanying music, he became stuck 50 feet off the ice directly above the Ducks home goal. While the staff worked feverishly to free him he hung there, swinging gently to and fro, as the crowd went nuts. All through the pregame show, and even when the officials came on to the ice, he hung there helplessly, giving new meaning to the term "suspended animation."

Soon the two teams made their entrance. Goalie Guy Hebert, leading his Mighty Ducks teammates onto the ice, did a classic double take when he spotted the gigantic duck hovering directly over his net. Having solved the mechanical problem, the crew slowly reeled Wild Wing back up into the rafters just as the National Anthem began. It was indeed memorable, if not moving, to see fans standing at attention with their hands over their hearts as if participating in some odd kind of feathered flag raising ceremony.

Going from the frying pan literally into the fire, Wild Wing nearly became roast duck when he tried unsuccessfully to leap over a flaming obstacle during a pregame show. The plan called for Wild Wing to race toward a small, circular trampoline located at center ice. Leaping onto the trampoline, he would then be propelled over a 3-foot-high wall of flame and land safely on the other side, all to the anticipated thunderous applause of the crowd. Did I mention he would be doing this on ice skates?

In the days prior to game night, Wild Wing practiced the routine over and over again, each time performing it with ease. Of course, it was deemed unnecessary to practice it with the actual fire, what with all those smelly gas fumes and smoke. Surely the mere presence of fire wouldn't change anything, right? Right.

The night of the actual performance, excitement was in the air. Nothing like a death-defying leap through flames to get the crowd into the game. As the lights dimmed and Wild Wing made his descent, a flurry of

*Wild Wing, the Mighty Ducks' mascot, has provided the Anaheim crowd with a lot of entertainment, some of it at his own expense.*

> The giant duck became known as "Wild Wing," a name it would live up to in ways no one would have predicted.

activity was clandestinely taking place on the ice surface below. The trampoline was positioned at the center ice face-off circle and approximately three feet beyond it, a gas-powered barbecue big enough to handle a side of beef was moved into position. What none of us knew then was that it was also big enough to handle a huge duck.

Finally on the ice, Wild Wing skated to his mark and awaited the lighting of the fire. As is characteristic of propane, its ignition usually starts with a sudden burst of flame, and this was no exception. Not only did the crowd gasp, but the duck seemed to recoil as well. Hesitantly starting toward the trampoline, then stopping and backing up, he looked to be having second thoughts about what was once thought to be a simple stunt, but now looked more like what had made Evel Knievel famous.

Urged on by the cheering masses, Wild Wing finally began skating towards liftoff. While experts would later argue that the big duck lacked sufficient terminus speed, it was clear from the moment he jumped onto the trampoline he was going to fly in, not over, the flames. Doomed when his skate got caught in the trampoline's frame, Wild Wing pitched forward and landed right in the middle of the fire. Held down by the weight of his costume, he thrashed around trying to free himself, only adding fuel to the flame. As the smell of burning feathers wafted into the stands, Wild Wing was pulled from the flames by his ground crew, whose speedy reactions were the only thing that kept him from becoming Duck Flambe. The fans loved it.

Given the warm reception by the fans to stunts involving flames, another entertaining routine involving fire was cleverly scheduled to be performed prior to a game between the Mighty Ducks and the Calgary Flames.

Noting the even warmer reception received by the duck, it was wisely decided that no actual flames would be used in this particular production.

The program involved a skater dressed as a Calgary player entering the rink with an empty gas can pretending to dump imaginary gas on the Ducks players' bench and goal, all done to the disco song, "Burn, Baby, Burn." Coming to the rescue of the Mighty Ducks, Wild Wing would ride into the rink on the back of a real fire engine and scare the firebug away.

With Wild Wing playing the role of rescuer, and not being near any open flames, there was certainly no need to actually practice driving the vehicle onto the ice, what with all those smelly exhaust fumes and smoke. Surely, a huge City of Anaheim fire engine would fit through the Zamboni entrance, right? Right.

The show began as planned with the crowd in rapt attention as the skater did his part by quite realistically simulating an act of arson. With lights flashing, siren wailing, and Wild Wing standing on the back waving to the cheering fans, the fire truck started through the opening onto the ice and to the rescue. Unfortunately, about halfway through, it was discovered that Zambonis are a lot narrower than fire engines. Wedged tightly half on, half off the ice, the fire engine sat motionless as Wild Wing gamely continued waving to the crowd. Eventually realizing that the fire truck could not be driven onto the ice, cooler heads prevailed, the stunt was aborted, and Wild Wing began to climb down from the back. At that precise moment, the driver, demonstrating that the right wing didn't know what the left wing was doing, put the machine into reverse and began to back up. Only the duck's quick-thinking handlers saved it from being road kill. The fans loved it.

Small wonder that Wild Wing continues to amuse the crowd to this very day. But with a few more stunts like these, they may be serving him *a la carte* at the concessions along with the pizza and hot dogs.

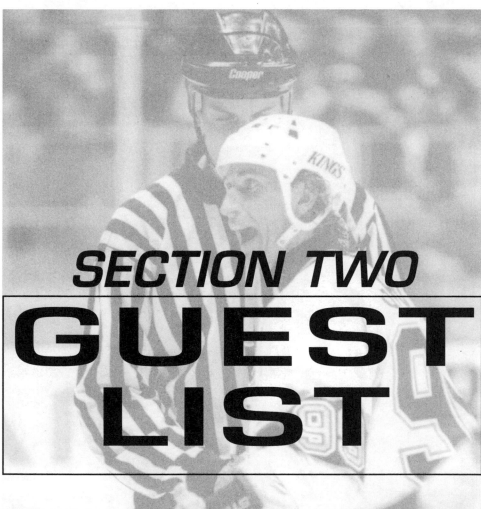

*SECTION TWO*

# GUEST LIST

# Icing

## Caring for Penalty Box Guests

There is one thing I can nearly always count on when working the penalty box: I won't be alone. Much rarer than a scoreless tie is the game in which no penalties are called. Therefore, it's a safe bet that in every game I'll have at least one visitor, even if only for a couple of minutes. Because my guests are looking for something other than a firm mattress and a continental breakfast, special preparations are done to each of the penalty boxes prior to the opening face-off.

Rink attendants begin by mopping the rubberized floor of each of the boxes to remove any debris that might have entered the box courtesy of fans who use it to express their innermost feelings about the penalized player and his misdeed. A particularly aggravated penalty, such as winning a fight against a hometown favorite, or just being Theoren Fleury, can result in a barrage of items ranging from foodstuffs to souvenirs. In the case of Theoren Fleury, the attendants forget the mops, and go directly to a skip loader. Keeping the floor clean can become an act of self-preservation. I can only imagine the carnage that would follow if Chris Simon was to step out of the box and fall down because a piece of gum got stuck on his skate blade.

Next the door latch is tested to ensure the gate can be opened on time. Worse than letting a player out early is keeping one in too long. Granted, they're both problems, but one results in being locked in with a real angry guy standing over you who's holding a big stick in his hands.

Extremely important is the placement of several squeeze-type water bottles in various locations throughout the box. Whether serving time for a minor or major penalty, players' first reaction when entering the box is to reach for the squeeze bottles filled with chilled water. Research seems to suggest that hydration both before and during physical activity restores energy, and players waste no time in refilling their tanks. Not only does it replenish fluids lost through perspiration, but for many players it fuels what has become an art form: spitting. If this talent could be harnessed and done only during the between-period intermissions, they could do away with the Zambonis.

Also placed in the box for the players' use are several rolls of tape in team colors, and towels, towels, and more towels. On any given night there are probably enough towels on hand to dry up Lake Superior. And in the not-so-rare instance of bloodletting, rubber gloves and disposable bags similar to those used for discarding nuclear waste are available for removing the ravages of war.

In general, these items are pretty harmless, nondescript stuff. There is, however, one item routinely put in every penalty box in the league that must be completely hidden from view. Like the Cross to Dracula, seeing it can cause the toughest of the tough to shrink back in horror. Its mere mention can cause a startling range of emotions, from embarrassment to rage. Of course, I'm talking about the ice bag.

The two most frequently asked questions by players after receiving five minutes for fighting are, "Am I bleeding?" and "Will I need stitches?" Unfortunately, the answer to both questions is usually "yes." The question that *should* be asked most frequently under the same circumstances is, "Do you have an icebag?" But while that's the most obvious question, it's also the rarest.

Home medical remedy manuals typically list a whole bunch of maladies for which the use of ice is recommended as a means of treatment. Most of them are the kind that directly result from hockey fights. Annoying little problems like black eyes, bruises, contusions, and nosebleeds. So, why would a player in need of the icebag refuse to ask for it? Well, it has little to do with pride and a whole lot more to do with the many reasons hockey fights generally occur in the first place.

Contrary to the opinion of some, not all fights occur because one player is angry with another. More often than not, fighting is a means of pumping

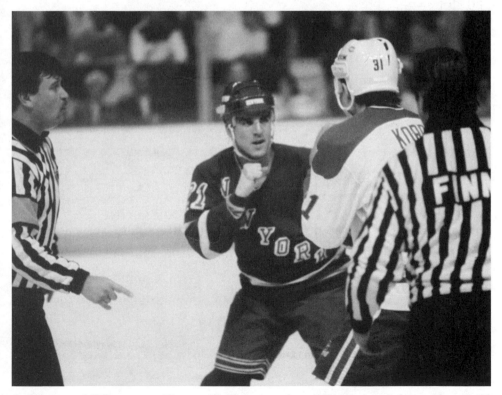

*In his seven NHL seasons, George McPhee earned a reputation as a player who would "show up" at crunch time.*

**One item is routinely put in every NHL penalty box that must be completely hidden from view.**

up a team that's flat. In almost every case these fights involve the respective team's tough guys, and are usually agreed upon in advance by both participants. One player says, "You wanna go?," and the contest is on.

A fair amount of fights take place because a player has taken liberties with an opponent who is considered untouchable, such as a star player or any goalie other than Ron Hextall, who has demonstrated on more than one occasion that he can take care of himself just fine, thank you. I'm sure Chris Chelios would wholeheartedly agree with that assessment.

Early in Wayne Gretzky's career, it was thought to be an unspoken rule not to get physical with him because he was the league's drawing card. Before a game with Edmonton, one league tough guy said he didn't care who Gretzky was, he was going to play the body. After a typically big offensive night for the Great One, the player was asked why he didn't check Gretzky. His classic answer was, "You can't check what you can't catch." Of course catching Wayne Gretzky meant getting past a whole bunch of his defenders, chief among them being big, bad Dave Semenko, whose specific job it was to make sure no checks were cashed at Wayne's expense.

Some fights take place because one player is literally fighting for a roster spot, and, again, they usually involve challenging an opponent of equal or better fighting skill. Picking a fight with a smaller, less physical player would likely result in a roster spot in a men's beer league, regardless of the outcome.

Once a challenge is issued, not backing down is a sure way to endear a player to his team and to the fans, and garner respect from other players around the league. When then-Ranger George McPhee (5' 7", 170 pounds) accepted the challenge of then-Flyer Dave Brown (6' 5", 222 pounds), he solidified his reputation as a man who could be counted on to "show up" when needed. Players who back down or "turtle" quickly earn a reputation as someone who can be intimidated, and in a game as physical as NHL hockey, this would likely lead to extended stays on the injured reserve list or even the end of a career.

Regardless of the reason a fight starts, when it's over, both combatants need to look like the winner, and there's no room in that picture for the ice bag. As a result, when they come in the box after a main event, I don't even ask anymore if they want the ice bag. I simply toss it under the bench where they're sitting and let them make their own choice.

It is ironic that in no other sport does ice play as prominent a role as it does in hockey. Players at this level have spent years honing their considerable skills by practicing and playing on 17,000 square feet of it. They're as much at home on the ice as we are on *terra firma*. But put a little in a plastic bag and offer it to them, and they'll give it the cold shoulder every time.

# Guilt by Association

## Cleansing the Soul and Helping with the Paperwork

Being a referee or linesman in the National Hockey League is as gruelling as it gets. Long before they get on the ice, they have to get to it. Their travel schedules keep them in the air so much, they could buy Kansas with their frequent flyer miles. When they arrive at the rink, they have to be in better condition than an Olympic athlete to perform their unique type of triathalon: skating a ton of miles, breaking up toe-to-toe battles, and causing thousands to go nuts simply by enforcing the rules. For this, they are paid a fraction of what is earned by the players they keep in check, and they do so in relative anonymity, since someone had the bright idea to take the names off their uniforms.

In the eighty year history of the National Hockey League, there have been thirteen referees and linesmen inducted into the Hall of Fame. Names like Armstrong, Chadwick, D'Amico, and Pavelich are almost as familiar to hockey fans as are the names Cournoyer and Mikita. Imagine what the announcement will be like if and when one of the current crop of On-Ice Officials makes it to that hallowed ground:

"The National Hockey League announced today that Referee Number 38 has just been voted into the Hockey Hall of Fame."

**Once the referee's whistle blows, there's paperwork to be done, and lots of it.**

I'm sure ol' 38's family and fans will be suitably impressed.

By design, officials should be anonymous and allow the game to continue with a minimum of stoppages. Otherwise, you have a slippery game of basketball. Calling penalties not only interrupts the natural flow of the game, but triggers a significant amount of behind-the-scenes activity. Once the referee's whistle blows, there's paperwork to be done, and lots of it. This becomes the primary responsibility of the Penalty Timekeeper who maintains a detailed record of the penalty, the time it was called, the recipient, and the time it expires, either through serving it in full or terminated by a power play goal. In extreme cases, such as a gross misconduct or match penalty, a special form is required by the league listing the details of the penalty, as well as the names and numbers of all players on the ice when the penalty occurred. This information enables the league to conduct an investigation to determine appropriate sanctions, if any, in the form of fines and/or suspensions. In most cases, the game is played with a minimum of whistling and writing, but there are notable exceptions. In fact, in one historic game, the paperwork generated probably cost the lives of at least two giant redwoods.

Take, for example, the game at the Spectrum on March 11, 1979, when the Los Angeles Kings came to do battle with the Philadelphia Flyers. The game started at 7:30, and the fisticuffs must have started at 7:31. How else could two teams rack up a record 372 penalty minutes in the first period? Los Angeles, tired of getting beaten by the Broad Street Bullies on the scoreboard and the ice, had picked up tough guy Randy Holt, and he didn't need to have it spelled out what his role was to be. What started out as a two minute minor turned into bedlam. Demonstrating that he took his new job seriously, Holt picked up 67 minutes in penalties, a record that stands to this very day.

For those of you keeping a record at home, here's the breakdown: 1 minor, 3 majors, 2 ten minute misconducts, and 3 game misconducts. Holt got more time than an ax murderer. Not to let the hometown fans down, the Flyers earned 4 minors, 8 majors, 6 ten minute misconducts, and 8 game misconducts for a total of 188 penalty minutes. Between the two teams they had 16 players tossed due to game misconducts. There were more players in the locker rooms than were on the ice. They almost had to hold the draft early just so they could get enough players to finish the game.

Anytime two teams decide to wage war, the action can get so wild, it's hard for the officials both on and off the ice to keep track of it all. And sometimes the refs have to rely on the players themselves to sort it all out.

*Enforcer Randy Holt (shown here as a Calgary Flame) holds the NHL record for most penalty minutes in a game.*

**PENALTY BOX**

**Randy Holt**
Games Played: 416
Total Points: 46
**Penalty Minutes:** 1,521

Following a multi-player melee on the ice at a Mighty Ducks game, several players were ushered into the penalty boxes while the referee (who shall remain nameless) read off the various penalties at the scorer's table. When he was through, there was a player sitting in my penalty box who hadn't been given a penalty.

"What's he in for?" asked the Penalty Timekeeper as he gestured to the unpenalized player sitting in the box.

"I don't know, but he must have a guilty conscience. So as long as he's in there, give him a minor for roughing, too."

# Fiery Flame

## Dynamite Comes in Small Sizes

In 1972, professional hockey skated into the Deep South when the National Hockey League granted a franchise to Atlanta, Georgia. Hoping to ensure the team's success, one of the sport's most recognizable names was hired as coach. Unfortunately, Bernie "Boom Boom" Geoffrion was only behind the bench, and not on it. Short of talent and long on travel, the Atlanta Flames lasted only eight seasons before the spark went out. Frequently facing younger, stronger, more talented teams, the travel-weary corps of mostly inexperienced or over-the-hill players struggled to win 268 out of 636 regular season games. The thrill of making the playoffs, which amazingly they did six out of eight seasons, was quickly doused when the Flames could only win two of seventeen playoff games.

To make matters worse, uncomplimentary comparisons to the other team that also began their National Hockey League existence in 1972 were unavoidable. While Atlanta was going down in flames in the preliminary round of the 1979–80 playoffs, the New York Islanders were winning their first of four consecutive Stanley Cup Championships. Disappointing performances and disillusioned fans set the stage for Nelson Skalbania, a successful Vancouver businessman with a burning desire to own a National

Hockey League team. With big plans and a wallet to match, Skalbania bought the franchise, and on June 24, 1980, began the history of the Calgary Flames.

Beginning play in an arena appropriately named the "Corral," the Flames responded immediately to knowledgeable and wildly enthusiastic fans. Through prudent coaching and player personnel changes, and fueled by a determined, supportive management, the Calgary Flames steadily progressed up the standings, finishing first in their division in 1987–88 only to be shut out 4–0 in the division final by their arch rivals: the dynasty-to-be Edmonton Oilers. As the 1988–89 season began, hopes were high that Calgary could break Edmonton's stranglehold on the Stanley Cup. To do so meant finding the missing piece that separates the winners from the also-rans, from those who drink to the Cup, but not out of it.

Theoren Fleury was born on June 29, 1968, in Ox Bow, Saskatchewan, and rumor has it he was then only slightly smaller than he is now. Despite being vertically-challenged, Fleury showed tremendous hockey ability and determination as a young player, enough so to be selected to play for Moose Jaw in the tough, physical Western Hockey League. During his four seasons with Moose Jaw, he scored 472 total points in 274 games. His scoring percentage is even better when you consider that while he was racking up those points, he was also spending the equivalent of almost ten games (551 penalty minutes) watching from the penalty box. In 1987–88, his last Western Hockey League season, Fleury tallied 68 goals and 92 assists for a league-leading 160 points, while spending 235 minutes in the custody of the penalty box timekeeper. The scoring numbers said a lot about his hands, but the penalty minutes said a whole lot more about his heart.

His play was good enough for the Calgary Flames to take him in the 1987 entry draft, but not until the 166th name was called. Right behind such future stars as Bryan Deasley, Kevin Grant, Scott Mahoney, Tim Harris, Tim Corkery, and Joe Aloi. At 5' 6" and 160 pounds, he continued

*Famously intense, Theoren Fleury is just as dangerous in the penalty box as he is on the ice.*

> With a linebacker's voice and a sailor's vocabulary, Fleury does his penalty time with the same intensity with which he skates his shifts.

to be labeled as too small to compete in a league with a fetish for "power forwards," big men who could muscle the puck out of the corners and themselves into the slot.

After a two-point-a-game pace in forty games with the Flames' International Hockey League affiliate in Salt Lake City, the little guy was brought up to the big club in hopes he could play a role in the final drive for the playoffs. He didn't disappoint. Following a dazzling regular season finish, Fleury scored eleven points in the playoffs, the most important one being the winning goal on Patrick Roy in Game One of the finals against the Montreal Canadiens. Driven by a Herculean intensity and monumental skills, Fleury was considered by many to be the missing piece that finally brought Lord Stanley's Silver Cup to the Flames, and in the process shattered the notion that a small man could not be a competitive force in the National Hockey League.

While no one who has ever been within earshot of Theoren Fleury would mistake him for royalty, his overall performance in the National Hockey League has been generally nothing short of majestic. A fifty-goal scorer with four seasons at or near a hundred points, his leadership both on and off the ice led to him being named captain of the Flames. His 1995–96 season ranks as the best ever in Flames history. That season, Fleury led his team in goals, assists, points, plus/minus rating, power play goals, short-handed goals, and shots on goal.

Watching Theoren Fleury make the pretty play is exhilarating, but seeing him make his way to the penalty box strikes terror in the hearts of Off-Ice Officials everywhere. Hated by the same fans who would give anything to have him play on their team, his penalties are greeted with cheers usually reserved for hometown hat tricks. With a linebacker's voice and a sailor's vocabulary, Fleury does his penalty time with the same intensity with which he skates his shifts, causing normally law-abiding fans to shower the penalty box with expletives and anything they can get their hands on. Sitting next to him in the penalty box without a helmet on can be a life-threatening experience.

During one particularly close game between the Mighty Ducks and Calgary, Fleury was given a minor penalty late in the game with the Flames trailing by a goal. Outraged to the point of mania, Fleury launched a withering barrage of insults directed at the On-Ice Officials as well as their ancestors. I watched with growing trepidation as the linesmen forced him towards and into my penalty box. Undaunted, he continued his animated verbal attacks on the officials, who ignored him as they skated away, leaving the two of us together and alone.

Sensing impending harm, I backed as far into the corner of the box as I could, irrationally hoping he would somehow not realize I was there. Rather than diminish, his anger towards the officials reached a new crescendo when his penalty was announced to the approving roar of the crowd. Then, slowly, as though drawn by some inaudible signal heard only by him and animals, he began to turn in my direction. Now facing me as I cowered in the corner, I could see him staring towards, but not at me. His eyes were lower, focused on my chest, focused on the NHL logo on my blazer. Standing there holding his stick like a pitchfork, he seemed to be glaring at the logo I had so proudly paraded past family and friends. The logo that never met a mirror it didn't like was about to cause my hospitalization.

Before I could remind him in a quavering voice that it's a match penalty to assault an official, he

## PENALTY BOX

### Theoren Fleury
Games Played: 790
Total Points: 823
**Penalty Minutes:** 1,367

spotted the chair I keep in the box. In a flash, he speared it with his stick and lifted it into the air. Swinging it over his head like a lariat, he flung it against the back wall, where it collapsed in a twisted heap. Understand this is no ordinary folding chair. Made of heavy gauge steel with a thick padded seat, it weighs in at just over twelve pounds, and despite its ungainly shape, it flew through the air like a guided missile.

Satisfied he had made his point, Fleury finally took a seat on the bench from where he bellowed continuous instruction and encouragement to his outnumbered teammates, while seemingly oblivious to the torrent of food and paper goods being hurled into the box. Without warning, an overzealous fan jumped on the glass at the back of the box and yelled some unintelligible but clearly hostile remark. Without looking, Fleury immediately swung his stick over his head in a reverse tomahawk and smashed it against the glass behind him, narrowly missing the now terrified fan's hands.

In a storybook finish, Calgary scored to tie, and scored again in overtime to pull out the win. Both goals happened while Fleury was still in the box, and each caused him literally to leap off the bench screaming and smash headlong into the glass. I couldn't open the door fast enough, and as he skated away, I felt a great sense of relief that Calgary had won that game. Had they lost, chances were good I would have been found lying on the penalty box floor battered and broken like my chair.

Theoren Fleury is the heart of the Flames and intensity is at the heart of his game, so you can be sure I'll be seeing him back in the penalty box going wild again for what he feels is another bad call by the officials. But I've come up with a foolproof way to feel safe. I just don't know how stupid I'll look wearing my blazer inside out.

# Profane Wayne

## Turning Lady Byng's Face Red

No other athlete, professional or amateur, male or female, has dominated a sport as has Wayne Gretzky. His accomplishments are legend not only to avid hockey fans, but to those who think a puck really does leave a red rocket trail when being shot. Holder of more than 60 National Hockey League records, he may very well skip the Hall of Fame and go directly to Sainthood. A quick glance at the record book and one would think Gretzky's nickname should have been Most: Most assists in a road game, Most goals in a period, Most short-handed goals in a playoff game, Most, Most, Most.

It's not only the number of records that makes Wayne Gretzky the Great One. It's the ease with which he broke existing records that were themselves considered unbreakable. Gretzky didn't just slip past Phil Esposito's record 76 goals, he obliterated it with 92. The National Hockey League record book lists the ten all-time highest single season assist totals, and Number 99 is number one with a whopping 163. Gretzky's also second on the list. And third, fourth, fifth, sixth, seventh, eighth (tied), ninth, and tenth (tied). In fact, Gretzky has established a career record of assists that are more than the total points scored by any other player in the history of the National Hockey League.

As seemingly unbreakable as Wayne's records are, reality tells us that there will someday come another with the same unique blend of talent and commitment who will succeed in fulfilling his dream of being the Greater One. Despite the adage that records are made to be broken, there was a chance to set a record that would be so extreme, so beyond what had ever been accomplished before in the game of hockey, that Wayne Douglas Gretzky would be number one in the record books for as long as history is recorded. That opportunity came in my penalty box on April 9, 1995.

During the strike-shortened 1994–95 season, the Los Angeles Kings came to the Pond for the second of five meetings with the Mighty Ducks of Anaheim. Intensifying their crosstown rivalry was the fact that both teams were in imminent danger of missing the playoffs. Though the Ducks had the offensive punch of superstar-to-be Paul Kariya, they had continued to test the market for available defensemen who could play the body as well as the puck and point. On March 9, 1995, the Ducks picked up David Karpa from the Quebec Nordiques, hoping he was that player.

Over 6' and 200 pounds, the Regina, Saskatchewan native was a strong skater with a big shot and a chip on his shoulder—a combination that endeared him to the hometown fans and infuriated visiting players. His strength was in his ability to agitate, to take a player off the ice or out of a game not with his fists, but with his mouth. While teammates practiced plays, Karpa worked on the fine art of heckling. His chief skills were breakouts and insults. He was Henny Youngman with an attitude. Less than two weeks after he was acquired, the Grate One was about to match up with the Great One.

## PENALTY BOX

**Wayne Gretzky**
Games Played: 1,625
Total Points: 3,177
**Penalty Minutes:** 629

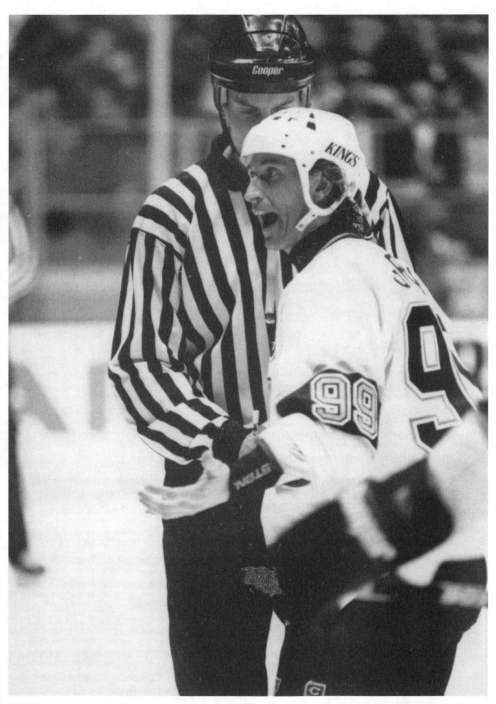

*While Wayne Gretzky's scoring talents are the stuff of legend, he has shown an ability to dish out the insults as well as the puck.*

Late in the first period, the Kings dumped the puck deep in the Ducks' end as Gretzky and Jari Kurri raced in to get possession. As Gretzky skated by, Karpa said something, then bumped him just hard enough to knock him off balance and into the boards. Smarting from the roar of the crowd as much as the fall, Gretzky immediately got up and skated toward Karpa who was now heading up ice unaware Wayne was planning a Duck shish kebab.

Video replays show that as he skated past Karpa, Gretzky jabbed him in the side with his stick. In a reflexive motion, Karpa swung his stick at Gretzky, missing, but simultaneously prompting a whistle from the referee and an attack by Marty McSorley. As Gretzky was directed towards my box, I glanced around at the fans sitting nearby, and their expressions told me they had the same thought I did. We were about to be in the immediate presence of the most famous and skilled hockey player in the world, a person for whom the title the Great One seemed almost too modest.

As he got closer, I could hear him talking to the linesman in a pleading, childlike tone of voice, asking whether Karpa was also getting a penalty. When the linesman told him the referee had only given a penalty to him, things got ugly real fast. Standing in the penalty box doorway, Gretzky began a stream of expletives that continued as he took his seat on the penalty box bench. His face contorted with anger, the childlike voice had now become a raspy snarl.

He seemed to pause only to inhale as he continued his litany of profanity, clearly audible to players, fans, and officials alike, for the entire duration of the penalty. At one point, the referee turned and looked in his direction, and Gretzky, staring straight at him, said, "Yeah, I'm talking to you, you #@%$^&."

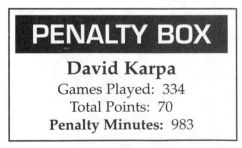

## PENALTY BOX

**David Karpa**
Games Played: 334
Total Points: 70
**Penalty Minutes:** 983

I began to reach for the penalty box door thinking the referee was going to give Gretz the gate, but he simply shook his head and turned away. Once again, I looked around at those seated near the box and, like me, they now had shocked and horri-

**Wayne's intensity is reflected in his play, and only rarely in his temper.**

fied looks on their faces. The only one who seemed to be enjoying this display was David Karpa, who kept skating close by and looking into the box with a big grin on his face, each time causing Gretzky to increase the tempo and intensity of his name-calling.

Even though I was too surprised to keep a running tabulation, I would estimate that Wayne used profanity at least fifty times. National Hockey League Rule 41(a) makes it clear that use of any profanity will result in a ten minute misconduct penalty being assessed. Had Rule 41 (a) been applied to each incidence of profanity, the Great One would have amassed over 500 minutes in penalties . . . in one game. Characteristic of his other record-breaking efforts, this would have eclipsed Randy Holt's single game record of 67 minutes by a mile. In comparison, tough guy Dave "Tiger" Williams, the all-time National Hockey League penalty minute leader only averaged a mere 4.12 minutes a game. And while Dave "The Hammer" Schultz had acquired 472 penalty minutes, it took him the entire season of 76 games to do it.

For a relatively small man to compete at the highest level in a sport as physically demanding and confrontational as hockey requires not only tremendous skill, but an intensity level incomprehensible to others. Most of the time, Wayne's intensity is reflected in his play, and only rarely in his temper. On this night, however, the Great One put on a show not seen before or since.

Though Wayne Gretzky is without a doubt the greatest scorer to ever lace on a pair of skates, it is equally without doubt that his scoring records will eventually fall, though possibly not in this millennium. But he came close to setting one record on that night in April which would never, ever have been broken.  I not only saw it; I heard every  #@%$^ &  word of it.

# The Big O

## It's Much Better to Give Than to Receive

History indicates that the Algonquin Indian migrated to the area of the Great Lakes as early as 2500 B.C., although the first detailed description of their culture begins in 1603 in the diary of a French historian charting the Great North. Regarded as a strong and fearless people who subsisted on trapping and hunting, their name literally translated means "they are our friends/allies."

They needed plenty of both. Besieged by continuing warfare with neighboring Mohawk and Iroquois tribes, and beset by measles and smallpox, their numbers had steadily declined from over 50,000 to fewer than 6,000. With a ferocious desire to survive and the guidance of their tribal spirit, *Wiskedjak*, the Algonquin migrated to Northern Quebec and established a reserve called Maniwaki, the "river desert."

Steeped in tribal ritual, the reserve and its approximately 1,000 members continue today much as they have for centuries. But one of its members, having learned to play hockey on the outdoor rinks of the reserve, now does his hunting and trapping in the National Hockey League.

Gino Odjick is a full-blooded Algonquin Indian who grew up idolizing the exploits of former Boston and Pittsburgh winger Stan Jonathon. That pretty much tells you everything you need to know about Gino's style of hockey. Jonathon, a player for whom the term "hard-nosed" was a statement of anatomical fact, ended his eight-year career with over 750 minutes in penalties, most of them from fights he usually won in a big way. At 6' 3" and 210 pounds, Odjick is bigger and stronger than Jonathon and has surpassed his boyhood idol's numbers with close to 2,300 penalty minutes in less than eight years in the National Hockey League. In the process he has become one of the most feared players in the game today. But does a man who has forcibly imposed his will on virtually every tough guy in the league have fears of his own? Is there some symbol, like the cross is to Dracula, that would make this powerhouse shrink back in terror? As I found out, there is, and it was right in my penalty box all along.

In the first game ever pitting the Ducks against the Canucks, Gino didn't waste any time starting and finishing a toe-to-toe slugfest. After the linesmen separated the fighters, Odjick skated casually to the penalty box, wearing a big, toothless grin as if to say this was all in a good day's work. Once in the box, however, he crumpled on the bench, hunched over and facing away from me as if he had just been kicked in the stomach. I stood there wondering if I should call for a stretcher when I thought I heard him faintly mumble something. I leaned closer, straining to hear over the roar of the crowd.

"Hey, can you help me?"

Not knowing exactly what to expect, I reluctantly answered, "Yeah, what do you need?"

Still hunched over and facing away from me he said, "See that water bottle on the ledge there? Pick it up and set it on the bench right next to me, ok?"

Figuring he was going to rinse some horrible wound I hadn't seen, I quickly grabbed the squeeze bottle and put it on the bench next to him. Still hunched over, he continued to give me exact directions on where to place it.

"Right there. No, over a little to the left. Now back a little."

When I finally got the bottle in the precise spot he wanted, he abruptly straightened up and snatched the bottle, not saying a word and acting as if what we had just gone through hadn't even happened.

*Gino Odjick, seen here pleading his case, is known for his sense of fair play as well as his toughness.*

> Does a man who has forcibly imposed his will on virtually every tough guy in the league have fears of his own?

As I stared at him with a quizzical look on my face, he turned and looked at me for the first time and said, "I just have a little superstition about water bottles." Here's a guy who's been in more fights than Ali, and a plastic water bottle has him terrified. Go figure.

Although primarily known as a brawler, Gino does have the ability to find the back of the net, usually by parking directly in front of it. In the 1993–94 season, his banner year with 16 goals and 29 points, he scored a Lemieux-like five game winners. Nevertheless, points are hard to come by when, like Gino, you spend almost as much time in the box as on the ice.

Midway through the 1996–97 season, the Canucks came to Anaheim ahead of the Ducks in the standings, looking to stretch their lead with a win. And Gino Odjick was on fire with a two-game point scoring streak. Ok, so *streak* may not be the right word, but you tell him that. Early in the game on one of Gino's infrequent shifts, Vancouver scored after a scramble in front of the net.

As the Canucks were celebrating their goal, Odjick could be seen animatedly talking to the referee. Skating closer to me, I could hear Gino arguing that he should get an assist on the goal, but the referee wasn't buying it. Having no luck with the referee, he tried everyone within earshot, including, but not limited to, the official scorer, the penalty timekeeper, the scoreboard clock operator, an usher, and a half dozen or so fans. He even skated by my penalty box with a pleading look on his face as if I could in some way influence the decision. I gave him my patented blank stare, but that didn't seem to phase him a bit.

Soon enough the period ended, but when the players took the ice for the start of the next period, Gino skated right up to my open penalty box door, and asked if there was any change in the scoring to add an assist to him. As diplomatically as I could, I said that the Official Scorer reviews every goal before the decision

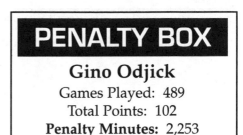

**PENALTY BOX**

**Gino Odjick**
Games Played: 489
Total Points: 102
**Penalty Minutes:** 2,253

becomes final, and that if there was any change it would come at that time. Seemingly satisfied with that, Gino skated off to the players' bench.

Later in the game, Gino picked up another penalty, and he no sooner hit the penalty box bench when he asked, "Any luck on getting that helper?"

"No, Gino, but they'll be sure to review it upstairs"

"Well, I sure hope I get it. That'll make the tribe back home happy, and, hey, it's not like I get a whole lot of those."

Unfortunately for Gino, an official review of the play failed to show he had assisted on the play, and his scoring "streak" ended at two games. True to his character, Gino fought for that assist with the same persistence with which he fought on the ice. Like his on-ice battles, he was at all times fair about it and accepted the decision once rendered.

In the modern era of hockey, where players' contracts contain complex incentive clauses based on a variety of performance factors, such as the awarding of goals and assists, plus/minus numbers, and even shots on goal, the Official Scorer's decisions come under intense scrutiny. In some cases, the awarding of these credits can make or break a player's career or determine whether he will be playing in the National Hockey League or the minors.

Gino cannot be faulted for arguing his case, but should be applauded for doing it in a gentlemanly manner. And I'm sure a lot of players around the league would be happy to have Gino settle his future disagreements in the same way: with his mouth, not his fists.

# Marty Mac

## The Prime Sinister of Hockey

Being traded means more than packing and plane tickets. Among other things it means being the new kid on the block who must prove himself to his new teammates. This process can usually be skipped by an established player whose reputation is widely known throughout the league. Take Marty McSorley. In his fourteen-year National Hockey League career, five different teams have done just that. Two of them even took him twice.

Strictly a brawler when he was originally signed as a free agent with Pittsburgh in 1982, he quickly established himself as a 6' 1", 235-pound force to reckoned with. His role didn't change from the one he had as a kid playing for the Belleville Bulls of the Ontario Hockey League: Play D with an attitude and show up at crunch time. But after only two seasons with the Penguins, Marty was included in a trade that would eventually bring him fame and fortune, with a couple of Stanley Cup rings thrown in for good measure.

Arriving in Edmonton for the 1985–86 season, McSorley set about making his mark on a team stacked with superstars and future hall of famers. His 315 penalty minutes in 67 games that first year made it pretty

> Marty Mac was an
> established tough guy
> who could be relied upon
> to "show up," and
> usually in ill humor.

easy to decide which player would inherit Dave Semenko's job of looking out for Number One.

Piling up penalty minutes came with ease, but it also came with a price. In all his years in the league, Marty has only played a complete season once. Every other one has been cut short due to injuries resulting from the aggressive style of play that has become a Marty Mac trademark.

McSorley's medical problems read like the Table of Contents to *Gray's Anatomy*. Abdominal muscle tear, ankle sprains and bruises, assorted knee injuries, shoulder injuries, rib cage injuries, bruised thighs. This guy has probably spent more time getting X-rays than penalties.

Traded to Los Angeles in 1988 with Gretzky and Mike Krushelnyski, he was originally included as a bodyguard more than a rear guard. Eventually moved up from defense to winger, he had his biggest offensive year ever when he scored a total of 51 points (19-32-51, including the playoffs) in the 1992–93 season.

Just so nobody got the idea he had gone soft, he also led the National Hockey League that season with a total of 459 minutes in penalties. It's numbers like these that explain why Marty is ranked as fifth all-time in penalty minutes with just a few main events shy of 3,600.

When traded back to Pittsburgh at the start of the 1993–94 season, Marty Mac was an established tough guy who could be relied upon to "show up," and usually in ill humor. During a game with the Ducks, he apparently wanted to make sure that fact hadn't been forgotten.

One of the first games ever played by the new Mighty Ducks of Anaheim was a preseason tune-up against the Pittsburgh Penguins and

*Ranked fifth all-time in penalty minutes, Marty McSorley is no stranger to the sin bin.*

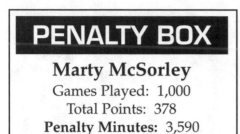

## PENALTY BOX

**Marty McSorley**
Games Played: 1,000
Total Points: 378
**Penalty Minutes:** 3,590

the recently acquired McSorley. The Ducks had a tentative roster full of players who were hoping to either start or extend their National Hockey League careers by making the team. Many, including tough guys Todd Ewen, Stu "The Grim Reaper" Grimson, and Jim Thomson, were prepared to battle their way onto the team, and McSorley would be the perfect opponent to showcase their skill and desire. Unfortunately for them, Marty Mac had an agenda of his own.

Before the end of the first period, Marty had picked up a fighting major and a roughing minor. The second and third periods were more of the same, with Marty picking up two more minors, and getting into another scrap that sent him back to the penalty box for another five minutes. McSorley was soon joined by Peter Taglianetti, sent in on a two minute minor. Once in the box, Taglianetti leaned over and said, "Hey, Marty, why all the penalties?"

"I just want the guys to know I'll show up, that they can count on me."

With an incredulous look on his face, Peter said, "Geez, I think everyone knows that."

After Taglianetti left, I jokingly told Marty if he got any more penalties, I was going to get a chair in the box with his name on it.

"No need, man. I'm not taking any more penalties. I've made my point."

With those words still ringing in my ears, Marty's penalty expired and I opened the door. No sooner had he stepped onto the ice than he and Robin Bawa became entangled, resulting in a ten minute misconduct for each and a free pass to the showers for McSorley. Another twenty-six minutes in penalties to prove a point already understood: You can count on Marty McSorley, and usually in two, five, and ten minute increments.

# Fighting Your Way *Out* of the NHL

## Playing with Heart

On December 22, 1995, the Vancouver Canucks and the Mighty Ducks met at the Pond in a game billed as one that would likely determine their future pecking order. With the Canucks attempting to regain their status at the top of the division, and the Ducks hoping to make a move towards the playoffs, the stage was set for a classic hockey game. One that would hinge on the character and toughness of the players, both as individuals and as a team. What wasn't known before the puck dropped that night was that a ninety-second fight would not only greatly influence the outcome of the game, but perhaps the National Hockey League future of one of the players.

Denny Lambert began his professional career in the 1990–91 season as a twenty-year-old left wing playing for the Sault Ste. Marie Greyhounds, the same team that more than twelve years earlier had been the showcase for another newcomer: Wayne Gretzky. While Lambert's offensive production was somewhat less than the Already Great One (67 points to 182 points), there were other numbers much more indicative of what Denny brought to the game. Numbers like 200 pounds and 169 penalty minutes. Although his weight would stay around the same rock-hard 200, his penalty minutes would steadily climb to 229 the next year, to 286 in 1992–93.

By the 1993–94 season, Denny was literally tearing them up in the International Hockey League, playing for the Ducks' minor league affiliate San Diego Gulls. His point production had dwindled considerably (27), but in 79 games that season, he posted 314 penalty minutes. These were not clutch-and-grab type penalties, but were instead earned blow-by-blow, stitch-by-stitch. The Ducks saw in him what every one of Denny's coaches had also seen: though not fleet of foot nor accurate of shot, he had a heart like a tractor, and a punch like a mule. It would be fair to say that Denny Lambert literally fought his way from Wawa, Ontario, into the National Hockey League. The Ducks decided to bring him up to the big show for the 1995–96 season. His role was both simple and familiar: to be a physical presence, to protect the scorers, to muck and grind.

In the 1989–90 season, another Ontario product had appeared on the professional hockey scene. Playing right wing for Hamilton of the Ontario Hockey League, Alek Stojanov immediately made his substantial presence known, and at 6' 4" and 225 pounds, his presence became known not only on the ice, but in the league's penalty boxes. Accumulating 286 penalty minutes in his first 99 games, Stojanov caught the attention of the Vancouver Canucks, who made him their first round, seventh overall pick in the 1991 entry draft. While he could score the odd goal, Alek was not sought as a replacement for high-scoring Trevor Linden, but more as a stablemate of tough Sergio Momesso.

## PENALTY BOX

**Alek Stojanov**
Games Played: 9
Total Points: 0
**Penalty Minutes:** 243

From the opening face-off on, the game was played at a furious pace, each team refusing to fold under the other's pressure. Midway through the first period, Lambert and Stojanov collided at center ice while

*Tough guys like Denny Lambert know that you're only as good as your last fight.*

> The fortunes of the tough guy lie in his ability to protect others, and to stimulate the team by throwing his weight around.

chasing a loose puck. In any other game, such a hit would more than likely be ignored, but on this night it was taken by both as an unmistakable challenge, a challenge that absolutely could not be ignored. In a flash, gloves and sticks were simultaneously dropped as each began to throw bombs. Lambert swung wildly, and Stojanov caught him flush on the jaw, buckling his knees. Giving up nearly six inches in height and 35 pounds, Lambert became the receiver of a torrent of punches that stunned, but did not drop him. Suddenly, and amazingly, Stojanov literally picked up Lambert and flung him in a heap to the ice, bringing a deafening roar from the capacity crowd.

The linesman guided Lambert to the home penalty box, where he sagged to the bench. More than beaten, he had been humiliated by the one-sidedness of the fight and its embarrassing finale. As he sat dazed on the bench, he kept repeating, "This was the worst fight I've ever had."

Looking at him, I was moved by the agony he was in over such a devastating and public loss. Out of sheer compassion, my mind frantically searched for something to say to him that might console him. I glanced into the visitor's penalty box as if I might see something there that would help me, but all I saw was the victorious Stojanov adjusting gear loosened from his nonstop delivery of punches. Suddenly, I thought of the one thing that might help to lessen Lambert's embarrassment and restore his confidence.

With as much bravado as I could muster, I said, "Hey, Denny, don't feel so bad. He's probably over there bleeding plenty."

Without hesitation, he dejectedly shot back, "Yeah, where? On his knuckles?"

Undoubtedly buoyed by the lopsided victory in this battle of the titans, Vancouver went on to win the game, and soon after, Denny Lambert was sent down to the Baltimore Bandits of the American Hockey League.

The role of a tough guy or "goon" is a limited one. Absent the scoring talent of a "skill" player, the fortunes of the tough guy lie in his ability to protect others, and to stimulate the team by throwing his weight around. Many observers feel that this was his only shot at the big time, but one thing is certain: Denny Lambert will put up one hell of a fight to get back into the National Hockey League!

## Postscript

Denny Lambert was sent down to the Baltimore Bullets after no goals, 8 assists, and only 55 penalty minutes in 33 games with the Mighty Ducks. Determined to make it back into the National Hockey League, Lambert went on a tear in the final 44 regular season and 12 minor league playoff games establishing his customary penalty minutes (165) while scoring at nearly a point-a-game pace (17-37-54). Hard work, a Lambert forte, paid off on July 29, 1996, when the Ottawa Senators signed him as a free agent.

Since the 1996-97 season, Denny Lambert has been an important part of the Senators' steady climb out of the National Hockey League cellar and into the playoffs. Of course, he still doesn't put a lot of points on the board. Ottawa has guys like Alexei Yashin and Daniel Alfredsson who take care of that quite nicely. But when the Ottawa fans are cheering, and the Corel Centre is rocking, it's as likely for a Lambert check as it is for some hot shot's blast from the blue line.

**PENALTY BOX**

**Denny Lambert**
Games Played: 215
Total Points: 52
**Penalty Minutes: 554**

# Slamnesia

## A Forgettable Main Event

Perhaps no single issue has divided hockey fans as intensely as that of fighting. Attempts to eliminate it have been largely unsuccessful, as the yearly high number of fighting penalties can attest. Those wanting to abolish fighting argue that it detracts from the inherent gracefulness of the game, and sets a bad example for young fans already inundated on a daily basis with violence. These factors, they feel, dramatically limit the sport's popularity and acceptance. To others, fighting is an unavoidable yet relatively harmless part of a game of skill and intimidation played in the fast forward mode. Fighting is a cathartic release of pent-up emotions, and the fans love it. The motto of advocates for allowing fighting is "no one goes for popcorn when a fight starts." Whatever one's position, it is clear that fighting is often not simply done for a spot on the ice, but for a spot in the lineup.

On a rare appearance by the New Jersey Devils at the Arrowhead Pond, the game had all the promise of an exciting, hotly contested game. The Ducks, perpetually struggling for a playoff spot, meant to make their move at the expense of New Jersey, a team determined to get their names back on the Cup. Both teams had made roster changes in an attempt to

> It was a shuddering crash, the kind punctuated with the loud, plastic crack of equipment.

strengthen the corps who hopefully would take them to and through the playoffs.

Among the players brought up by the Devils for the 1996–97 season was rugged forward Denis Pederson. Although taken in the first round, thirteenth overall in the 1993 Entry Draft, Denis had spent the first years of his pro career shuttling back and forth between the Devils in East Rutherford and their American Hockey League affiliate in Albany, with only a brief stop in Red Deer, Alberta, to help Team Canada win the 1995 World Junior Championship. To earn a spot with the Big Club, Denis knew the kind of game he had to play: drive to the net, and don't take the scenic route!

Like Pederson, Jason Marshall was also a first round draft choice, having been taken ninth overall by St. Louis in 1989. And like Pederson, he wanted no more minor league bus rides. Peoria, San Diego, and Baltimore were great places to visit, but Marshall didn't want his career to stay there. Two games with the St. Louis Blues were all that was needed to reinforce his dream of being a regular in the National Hockey League. But to remain with the Ducks, Coach Ron Wilson gave him specific directions: make the other team realize that the slot is a No Parking zone.

And so it was destined that at some point in the game these two players would arrive at the same place on the ice at the same time, and the result would be not only a violent collision of bodies, but a supreme test of wills.

The game started slowly, neither team able to penetrate the other's

## PENALTY BOX

**Jason Marshall**
Games Played: 179
Total Points: 22
**Penalty Minutes:** 379

*Understanding the strategic importance of a well-timed fight, Jason Marshall has never been afraid to drop the gloves.*

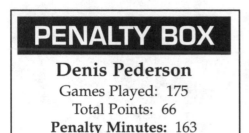

**PENALTY BOX**

**Denis Pederson**
Games Played:  175
Total Points:  66
**Penalty Minutes:**  163

defense. Time and again, one, then the other, would make an exciting rush, only to be repelled. Fueled by frustration, tempers grew short, then snapped. Charging through the slot in full stride and hunting for the rebound of a Scott Stevens' shot, Pederson came shoulder to shoulder with Marshall in a shuddering crash, the kind punctuated by the loud plastic crack of equipment. Stopped in their tracks and momentarily stunned by the impact, they glared at each other and, in an instant, the gloves were off and the battle was on.

A long fight by hockey standards, it began as a test of power, but became one of stamina. Weary from punching, the players would latch onto one another, continuing to awkwardly move around as if intentionally keeping the linesmen at bay, then begin again throwing punches too numerous to count and too painful to watch. Suddenly, both players slammed to the ice in unison as if each landed a haymaker at precisely the same instant. Exhausted more than injured, both were led to their respective penalty boxes.

Breathing heavily and totally spent from the endurance contest he had just been in, Pederson labored just to make it into the penalty box. I glanced over at Marshall who seemed to be in about the same condition. The fight having ended so abruptly made it nearly impossible to decide who had actually won. Both had thrown about the same number of punches, and neither had scored a knockout. As I found myself mentally replaying the fight and its uncertain finale to determine who, if either, had won, Denis abruptly turned to me and asked a question that simultaneously answered mine, "How did I go down?"

Dumbfounded by his question, I didn't have the heart or the nerve to tell him it's a pretty safe bet that the loser of a fight is the one who can't remember how it ended. It's also a pretty safe bet that with the determination and intensity shown by both of these players, neither will be riding the bus any time soon.

# Hands Off!

## Getting a Gameworn Jersey the Hard Way

Kris Draper doesn't know the meaning of the word *quit*.

Though not gifted with a scorer's touch or a power forward's size, he brings to the game something that can't be taught or learned. Heart. You either have it or you don't. His role is not to win games as much as it is to keep the other team from doing so. Backchecking and forechecking are the things he does best, and he does them relentlessly. Frequently he also gets the biscuit from the other guys and gives it to his own, with a determination that can irritate and infuriate. Unfortunately for Kris, there are other guys in the National Hockey League who have the same purpose, and who are sent out to beat him at his own game.

Some have tried to outmuck him, only to find he thrives in the corners. Shunning the relative tranquillity of the perimeter, Kris knows where to go, and what to do when he gets there. His mere 270 penalty minutes in 371 National Hockey League games shows that while he plays it tough, he also plays it clean. After all, Los Angeles King Randy Holt got 67 minutes in just one game.

Others have tried to bang with him only to learn the hard way that 185

> **Heart. You either have it or you don't.**

pounds at full speed is a force to be avoided. Especially when it keeps coming and coming and coming.

One guy even tried to take Kris out by cross-checking him from behind face-first into the boards. So blatant and vicious was this cheap shot, one down-on-his-luck fan in Draper's hometown of Toronto was seen carrying a sign reading:

"Will cross-check Claude Lemieux from behind for food"

True to form, Draper has turned injuries that would have ended most careers into just a temporary setback. Kris Draper doesn't know the meaning of the word *quit*. But fortunately for me, he does know when to stop.

Near the end of a grueling game between the Mighty Ducks and the Red Wings, tensions on both teams were reaching the boiling point. Another loss to the superior Detroit team was a bitter disappointment to the Ducks players, who had become increasingly chippy in their play as defeat loomed on the scoreboard. Hearing the mocking cheers at the announcement that one minute remained in the game was all that was needed to transform skating and shooting into pushing and shoving.

First Draper, then Keith Primeau, were sent with their Ducks dancing partners to their respective penalty boxes. As the final seconds on the clock ticked down, Draper and Primeau stood and moved to the penalty box door. Keith Primeau is a tall person to begin with, but add skates and he towers 6' 7" into the air, roughly a foot taller and about two feet wider at the shoulders than me. Not only did he block me from the penalty box door, but he also shielded my view of the ice. With the final horn sounding, I heard the click of the penalty box door handle at the same time that Mike Pons, the Penalty Timekeeper, yelled, "Don't let them out there."

What neither they nor I were aware of was that a scuffle had begun across the ice at the players' benches just as Draper and Primeau were

*Kris Draper's tough but levelheaded approach to the game has endeared him to his team-mates as well as confused Off-Ice Officials.*

**PENALTY BOX**

**Kris Draper**
Games Played: 371
Total Points: 89
**Penalty Minutes:** 270

about to step out onto the ice.

According to National Hockey League Rule 72, any player who leaves the penalty box during an altercation shall receive a game misconduct. But that's the least that happens. The first player to leave also is suspended for ten games without pay, and the second player to leave is suspended for five games without pay. Not wanting to test the application of this rule at the considerable expense of Draper or Primeau, and having to react quickly, I lunged forward and grabbed Draper's jersey at the shoulder as I yelled out, "Don't go out there."

He stopped dead in his tracks. For a moment, he stared straight ahead. What he must have seen that I couldn't was that the players, too exhausted to rumble, had given up and were filing into their respective dressing rooms. What he must have thought as I continued my death grip on his jersey was that an Off-Ice Official had just gone berserk. Ever so slowly, Draper turned his head and looked at my hand on his shoulder, and then, just as slowly, he looked up at me. He didn't have to speak a single word. The expression on his face told me in no uncertain terms that if I didn't move my hand now I would more than likely lose it. Even Primeau began to back up, apparently not wanting to get splattered with my blood.

I quickly took my hand away as I tried to explain in a halting voice why I had stopped him, an explanation he thankfully seemed to accept. But in the future, I've decided my health may depend on being able to keep my hands to myself. After all, I'd rather see him sit for ten games than me be hospitalized for weeks.

# Counting by Threes

## A Trio of Buffalo Take the Ice

The Buffalo Sabres National Hockey League franchise was established on May 22, 1970, and officially began play in the 1970–71 season. Although a coach extraordinaire, even George "Punch" Imlach couldn't get them into the playoffs. The next year brought even worse news in the form of still-standing club records for fewest wins (16) and fewest points (51) in a 78-game season. In their third season, the Sabres finally made an appearance in the playoffs, but that was only long enough to say hello before the Montreal Canadiens told them goodbye in the first round. At least showing consistency, they failed to make the playoffs again in their fourth season, and both management and fans became increasingly impatient with the lack of team progress.

The Buffalo Sabres started the 1974–75 campaign with dismal forecasts, but ended it tied with the Philadelphia Flyers for the lead in points with 113. The Sabres were paced by a trio of Frenchmen who delighted fans and terrified goalkeepers with their awesome skating, passing, shooting, and scoring.

Labeled the "French Connection" line, Gilbert Perreault, Rick Martin, and Rene Robert possessed individual skills that were admired by those

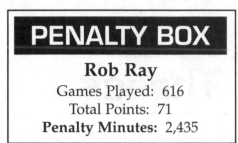

**PENALTY BOX**

**Rob Ray**
Games Played: 616
Total Points: 71
**Penalty Minutes:** 2,435

who simply watched the game and envied by those who played it. When combined with one another on the same line, the result was a march through the playoffs, eliminating Chicago and Montreal along the way, and leading to a showdown with the defending Stanley Cup Champion Flyers. Although losing in six games to the Flyers and Conn Smythe Trophy-winning goalkeeper Bernie Parent, the Sabres brought credibility to the organization and immortalized the contribution of three of its finest offensive players.

Fast forward to the start of the 1996–97 season. A new arena and new uniforms can't prevent fan discontent. After being eliminated in the first round two years in a row, the Sabres missed them completely in 1995–96. Pat LaFontaine, team captain and offensive star, is out indefinitely. Alexander Mogilny is a distant, and not too pleasant, memory. Reliable defenseman Richard Smehlik missed all of last year due to major knee surgery, and is still bothered by tendonitis. To top it off, the general manager is feuding with the coach. Not surprisingly, skepticism prevails. But here they are with three quarters of the season over, and the Buffalo Sabres are second in their division, fourth overall in the National Hockey League.

Enter Buffalo's latest hot trio: Rob Ray, Brad May, and Matthew Barnaby, each with a style of play that has immortalized them with the fans as well as penalty timekeepers around the league. In the 1995–96 season, the three sluggers combined for 917 penalty minutes, most by way of knockouts. Although capable of scoring, they terrorize other teams' tough guys more than their goalkeepers. Knowing they were coming to town to play the Ducks, I had two choices: double the number of towels and ice bags in the penalty box or double my life insurance. I did both.

Player One: Rob Ray is a generous man who has been known to give a guy the shirt off his back, usually after beating him to a pulp. A man of few words on the ice, once in the penalty box, he becomes as free with his talk as he is with his punches. Fighting his way to nearly 300 penalty minutes a season gives him plenty of time to develop his diction. Averaging about three goals a season over the last seven, Rob is clearly more effective ragging the puck than scoring with it, which has led to his rather unique theory of team selection.

After watching forwards doing a less-than-spirited job at backchecking, he once told me, "If I had my own team, I'd only have one forward on the whole squad. All the rest would be defensemen."

"Why would you have one forward?" I asked.

"Just in case we got a penalty shot!"

*Rob Ray, here discussing an on-ice infraction, is one of the great orators of the penalty box.*

> **The three sluggers combined for 917 penalty minutes, most by way of knockouts.**

Rob Ray, like his two soulmates, is a consummate team player who knows his role and executes it perfectly. He's not only essential on the ice, but in the locker room and on the bench. He contributes with his oratory as well as his work ethic.

Player Two: After missing most of the season, Brad May was back playing regularly, and that spelled trouble for visiting teams. Anxious to make a contribution, he holds himself to a high standard of play.

Brad picked up a minor penalty in a game against the Ducks, and joined Rob Ray, who was already serving time for impersonating Mike Tyson. As May sat watching the Ducks power play, Ray started in.

"Hey, Brad. The coach is gonna be upset with you if they score on your penalty."

"What about yours?"

"I brought someone with me," Ray countered.

And on it went, Ray ribbing May, who became progressively more worried as the penalty wore on and the Ducks rained shots on the Buffalo goalie. Groaning out loud with each Ducks shot, Ray kept up the needle, until I couldn't resist saying, "He's playing with your head, Brad."

Rob was loving it. "Brad worries about everything. We'll be out on the lake in the middle of summer with not a care in the world, and he'll be worrying about whether we'll catch fish, whether it's gonna start raining, whether the motor will start. You name it, he's sweatin' it."

When the penalty finally expired, May raced onto the ice, obviously relieved the Ducks had failed to capitalize on the opportunity he had given them.

**PENALTY BOX**

**Brad May**
Games Played: 488
Total Points: 179
**Penalty Minutes:** 1,423

Player Three: Matthew Barnaby has hands good enough to score series-clinching goals as well as main event knockouts. At 6" and 170 pounds, Barnaby's opponents are usually much bigger and stronger, but he is a heavyweight when it comes to heart and guts. With all the reason to go around traffic, Barnaby chooses to fight his way through it, which explains why he led the Sabres in penalty minutes with 335 in the 1995–96 season.

In the same game with the Ducks, Barnaby tried to force his way into the slot, and Ducks defenseman Jason Marshall tried to force him through the boards. Without a moments hesitation, "Barney" dropped the gloves, and the contest was on. Ending in a draw against a much bigger opponent wasn't acceptable to Barnaby, and he spent the entire time in the penalty box telling Marshall he wanted another go. Even though the penalties were interrupted by the break between periods, the first thing Barnaby did when he returned to the penalty box was yell over to Marshall, "Marsh, we're goin' again, right?"

Marshall had a look on his face as if to say, "When does this guy quit?" As many others in the National Hockey League have found out the hard way, he doesn't.

These three may not be the only reason Buffalo made a play to win it all in 1997, but each name on the Stanley Cup got there with the same kind of grit and determination this trio brings to every game. Imagine what kind of a team Buffalo would be if it had the French Connection line backed up by the three Ontario bad boys, Dominik Hasek, and some D thrown in for good measure. It might have been the very first Ice Dream Team.

**PENALTY BOX**

**Matthew Barnaby**
Games Played: 300
Total Points: 126
**Penalty Minutes:** 1,184

# A Nice Place to Visit, But . . .

## All Penalty Boxes Look Alike

The penalty box is not a hard place to find in a National Hockey League rink. Just watch guys like Enrico Ciccone, Paul Laus, Matt Johnson, Darren Langdon, Rocky Thompson, or Donald Brashear. Within minutes, they'll show you right where it is. For these guys, and players like them, the penalty box is their home away from home

Paul Kariya is not one of them. His forte is high speed action. He's much more at home scoring points. One-timer to him means a goal, not a knock-out punch. And talk about consistency. As an amateur playing for both the University of Maine and the Canadian National Team, he scored a total of 165 points and had only twenty penalty minutes. That's a ratio of 8.2 points for every penalty minute. Through his first three years as a pro, he scored 246 total points during the regular season, and had only thirty-penalty minutes during the same period. That works out to a ratio of points to penalty minutes of 8.2. As a comparison, Scott Daniels of the Philadelphia Flyers had 8 points and 237 penalty minutes in the 1996–97 season. His ratio works out to 29.6 penalty minutes for every point. Just like Kariya, Daniels fights for every point he gets, but in a slightly different way.

While it's obvious Paul doesn't spend much time in the penalty box,

> While it's obvious Paul doesn't spend much time in the penalty box, he should at least know where it is.

he should at least know where it is. After all, he's put a lot of his opponents in there who have had to haul him down while he's on a coast-to-coast excursion to their goal.

In one of his first National Hockey League home games, the Mighty One was assessed a two minute minor with less than a minute to go in the first period. Without argument, Paul immediately skated to the home penalty box and took a seat. When the horn sounded to end the period, I opened the door, and Paul skated directly to the Mighty Ducks' locker room. Following the intermission, I returned to the box, and as I entered, I left the door open in anticipation of Kariya's return to finish serving his penalty. After the warm-ups, Paul skated over to the home box, but rather than enter, he stood there with a quizzical look on his face. I approached him to see if there was a problem, and as I did so, he asked, "Do I finish up in this box or do I switch to the other one?"

Oddly enough, when a player the stature of Paul Kariya asks a question like that, it gives you pause. Hey, he's played hockey all his life, both at the college and international levels, and now in the National Hockey League. He was the most talked-about player to enter the league in years, and he's not sure in which box he finishes his penalty. For a moment you, too, begin to have doubts. Maybe he really is supposed to switch boxes at the start of the period, just like goalies who switch ends. Gee, maybe I'm supposed to be in the other box, too. Before I had a chance to look real, real stupid by leading both of us to the visitor's box, a voice rang out, "You stay in this box, Paul."

Having overheard Kariya's question, then watching me perspire without answering, the game scorekeeper had spoken up just in time to prevent

*Lady Byng Trophy Winner and all-around nice guy Paul Kariya's only shortcoming is his lack of penalty box knowledge.*

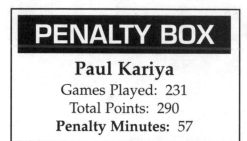

**PENALTY BOX**

**Paul Kariya**
Games Played: 231
Total Points: 290
**Penalty Minutes:** 57

major chaos. Paul didn't ask me any questions after that.

Recalling that night, I remember sitting next to him and thinking of the huge challenge that was ahead of him to make it in the National Hockey League. Lacking the overpowering size and strength of a Keith Primeau, he would have to be able to withstand rugged play that would undoubtedly be directed at him. Being basically a young man fresh out of college, the pressure had to be immense after being selected by Anaheim first, fourth overall, in the 1993 entry draft.

Judging by his size, he doesn't look as though he would be able to play a physical game, yet I have since seen him flatten Claude Lemieux, and bravely take a run at Darius Kasparaitis. His shots are as hard as they come, and his backhand may be the hardest and most accurate in the league. His superior speed is enhanced by near instantaneous acceleration. Listed at 5' 11" and 175 pounds, he has the stature of one who would be expected to play the perimeter, yet he intentionally steers into traffic. His ability to do this and survive the predictable bumps and bruises is due to a physical training regimen that is legend. And even though Paul Kariya has taught many a defenseman a lesson or two, he nevertheless still considers himself a student of the game, continually working on improving his play.

In the 1996–97 season, Paul Kariya's diligence and skill resulted in 99 points (44-55-99) in only 69 games, which placed him third among scorers despite missing 13 games. His penalties are so few and far between, he has won the Lady Byng Trophy two years in a row (1996, 1997). I suppose that's all well and good, but at this rate, how's he ever going to know where the penalty box is?

# Hey, LeClair!
# Where's My Puck?

## Acknowledging My First NHL Point

In 1987, a big boy from the little town of St. Albans, Vermont was playing defense at Bellows Academy when he got what must have been the greatest thrill of his young hockey life. He was selected 33rd overall in the second round of that year's Entry Draft by the most revered team in all of professional sports, the Montreal Canadiens. By the time he stepped from the rink at the University of Vermont onto the ice at the Montreal Forum for the 1990–91 season, he was 6' 3" tall, weighed 226 pounds, and had decided he liked the label "power forward."

It's almost impossible to imagine what John LeClair must have felt when he first entered the Canadiens' locker room, which has more the look of a shrine than a changing room. Beginning play in 1909, Le Club de Hockey Canadien has accumulated the greatest number of Stanley Cups with the greatest players the game has ever known. You may not have heard of Didier Pitre or Sprague Cleghorn, but the people at the Hockey Hall of Fame have. In fact, forty former Canadiens have been inducted with them into hockey's ultimate accolade, and they even got to bring along their old locker room. If the Canadiens retired the numbers of all the great players who have been on their rosters over the years, there wouldn't

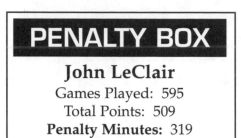

**PENALTY BOX**

**John LeClair**
Games Played: 595
Total Points: 509
**Penalty Minutes:** 319

be any numbers left to wear for the current team. They'd have to skate around using letters of the alphabet to identify themselves.

While LeClair may have been impressed, he certainly wasn't intimidated. He scored his first National Hockey League goal in his very first game. In his third season with Montreal, LeClair was a main part of their Cup-winning stretch drive, scoring back-to-back game winners in the finals at Los Angeles. In his fifth season, he was sent packing, but one of the things he took with him was his scoring touch. LeClair has scored 50 goals or more in each of the two complete seasons since that trade, and has been selected to the All-Star team every year thereafter. Something else I thought he would take with him when he left the Habs was a sense of tradition, but apparently I was mistaken.

When the Flyers came out during the pregame warm-ups, it was obvious the contest that night with the Mighty Ducks was going to be a very physical one. The "Legion of Doom" line consisting of Eric Lindros, Mikael Renberg, and LeClair averaged 6' 3" and had a combined weight of more than 675 pounds. Make that a half ton if you count Joel Otto (220 pounds) or Kjell Samuelsson (233 pounds). When a restaurant sees these guys show up for a pregame meal, they immediately begin slaughtering livestock. There was some question as to whether the rink could hold this much weight without collapsing. Watching these hulks skate around probably had some of the Mighty Ducks players hoping something like that would actually happen so that the game would be canceled. No such luck.

Actually, the Flyers really didn't have to play the body that night. Because of their size, they just seemed to skate in a direct line from point A to point B. If someone happened to be in the way, they just skated

*Bubble-gum chewing, goal-scoring John LeClair didn't acknowledge the author's timely assist.*

through and over them.

In the process of just such a move, LeClair was whistled off to spend two minutes contemplating his misdeed. What was immediately noticeable once in the box was that John didn't treat this like a rest period. He

> LeClair took one big step out of the box and landed in full stride with the puck right at his feet.

came in, sat down, and stared straight out at the ice, holding his stick the entire time as if he might get a pass while he was in the box.

His focus was so intense, it got me thinking this could be the moment I had been waiting for. I had often thought how great it would be to yank the door right on the money, and have the penalized player jump out, grab a loose puck, and race in for a quick score. Each time I pictured this happening, I would see the player, his stick raised in celebration while being mobbed by his teammates, turning and giving me the thumbs-up sign just as he steps over the boards. Sometimes when I would be replaying this in my mind after a couple of cups of coffee, I would imagine his teammates all banging their sticks against the boards as they also gave me the thumbs-up sign. I love caffeine.

As the penalty time on the Jumbotron counted down, I called out the time remaining, first at thirty seconds, than at fifteen. With that he was on his feet glancing rapidly back and forth from the play to the clock to the penalty box door. Feeling the pressure, my voice began to crack as I began counting down out loud from five. At the exact same instant I said "one," I pushed down hard on the handle and yanked the door so that it swung wide open just as the penalty expired.

LeClair took one big step out of the box and landed in full stride with the puck right at his feet. Before I could get the door shut, he was blowing in on Hebert at top speed. Just for a fraction of a second, I thought I could see the painted feathers on Guy's mask wilting. Coming into the net at an angle on Hebert's stick side, he pushed the puck forward as if looking for the backhander, but immediately pulled it back and fired it home for a goal. A huge roar went up from the crowd as LeClair coasted to his bench with his stick in the air.

I watched expectantly as he was mobbed by his teammates, and as he stepped over the boards he seemed to turn towards me, well, not exactly towards me, but sort of in the direction of the scorer's table, which is right next to the visitor's penalty box which is where I'm standing, you know. I thought it was right then that he made a nod or more like a real subtle shrug or something. I assumed he felt a little awkward about singling me out, and was probably going to do something special like, dare I say it, give me the puck he scored with.

And why not? Isn't that the age old tradition when a person gets his first NHL point? Even though it won't go in the record books as such, shouldn't I have gotten an assist on the play? Didn't I count down the time remaining without getting mixed up? Didn't I execute that tricky door-opening move with professionalism? Hey, he's good, but I'd like to see him score while still in the penalty box.

I was pretty confident that John, having played for the Montreal Canadiens and having learned the traditions of the National Hockey League from the team that virtually invented them, would recognize my first NHL point by handing over the biscuit. I waited around after the game, thinking maybe John might be looking for me, but I must have missed him.

It's been a couple of seasons now since that thrilling moment, and I still haven't received my puck. Even though I've pretty much given up hope for it, there has been something good that came out of it—I've cut way back on caffeine.

# SECTION THREE
# JOB
# ROTATION

# Time on My Hands

## Without a Degree from MIT

"We need you to run the scoreboard tonight, Lloyd."

Having just begun to get the hang of managing the visitor's penalty box, these were not words I wanted to hear from our supervisor, Tony Guanci. It had taken me several games to master opening and closing the penalty box door. That may sound like a simple task, but when you've got a 225-pound guy standing next to you snorting and stomping, wanting to get out, it can be very intimidating. And don't forget, you're also counting backwards. Out loud. This is a demanding job requiring great skill and concentration for which I'm paid a commensurate amount of money. Like, say, the parking lot attendants.

The players can make it very hard to be a major league door opener and closer, too. One time I was counting down, out loud, and when I got to three, the player standing in the box started banging his stick against the glass and yelling, "Come on, let's go. I need outta here. Open it up!"

Wadda guy. He's probably the type to yell "fire" in a crowded movie theater. Actually, he's probably the type to set a fire in a crowded movie theater. Then there's the other kind of guy, a guy like Joe Nieuwendyk.

> Virtually every device
> I had ever seen
> for turning something
> on and/or off was
> on this console.

Nearing the end of one of his infrequent penalties, he stood up and asked if I was going to open the door or should he. I was so appreciative of his courtesy towards me, I vowed the next time he came in, I was going to count down the entire two minutes. Out loud.

Well, I wasn't eager to take on this new job, even if it was only temporary, but being a team guy, I agreed to do it. Of course it did influence my decision somewhat that Tony had already disappeared down the hall, not interested in a debate on an issue he had already decided.

The scoreboard is in the scorer's booth, which sits between the home and visitor's penalty boxes in the middle of the rink and right smack across from Disney Chairman Michael Eisner's luxury suite. As I walked along the ice I remembered thinking this would not be the time or place to make a mistake. Blowing it in front of 17,174 fans was bad enough, but blowing it in front of The Man could very well have me singing duets with Iceman. Having put sufficient pressure on myself, I climbed into the booth for my first look at the scoreboard console.

I stood there stunned, the blood draining from my face. For a brief instant, I thought I had mistakenly stepped into the cockpit of a 747. I wondered if I was going to have to trade in my NHL blazer for a NASA suit. Toggle switches, dials, gauges, buttons. Everything but pedals. Virtually every device I had ever seen for turning something on and/or off was on this console. I'm sure somewhere in this maze of gadgetry were switches for the cargo doors and landing gear. What I hoped wasn't there was a switch for the house lights, or this game might end like the Edmonton/Boston playoff game a few years back: in total darkness.

Mike Carlucci, the Public Address Announcer tried to reassure me. "Don't worry, it looks a lot more complicated than it really is."

Right. It's only real complicated, not stupefyingly complicated. Before the game actually started, I was given a chance to familiarize myself with the control panel. I needed that time just to find out where I would be sitting. Soon enough, the game started, and there I was, trying to look relaxed, but worrying that my perspiration, now flowing in abundance, might drip onto the control panel and either short it out or electrocute me.

For some reason, I don't remember a whole lot about the game, which

*Media mogul and Head Duck Michael Eisner unveils his new team's logo and colors to the press.*

I'm told went pretty smoothly. Of course, there was that messy little problem when I tried to start the second period with 37 minutes on the clock, but I got that taken care of quickly. In fact, I don't think you-know-who even noticed.

And now that I know how to run the clock, I can't wait for that wise guy who tried to mess up my counting to come back and get another penalty. His two minutes might very well take all night to serve.

# You Be the Judge

## Just Sit There

At the time I was hired as an Off-Ice Official, I was told there was the strong likelihood that I would also work as a Goal Judge. While I enjoyed working in the penalty boxes, I was looking forward to doing this new job which I felt would be a lot less stressful, and would allow me to actually watch the game instead of only the penalty time clock. And besides, I wouldn't have to share my seat with the likes of Theoren Fleury.

This actually seemed to be a relatively easy job. I would get to sit in my own private booth, right on the glass and right behind the goalkeeper. I would have a perfect view of the ice, and would be able to see the whole show up close and personal, with nothing to do but watch the puck. When it crosses the goal line, push a button to turn on the red goal light. Big Deal.

It did occur to me that considerable time had elapsed since my last eye examination, so just to make sure my vision was up to speed, I set an appointment with my ophthalmologist, Dr. Clifford Terry. During the examination, I casually mentioned that I would be working as a Goal Judge at the Mighty Ducks games. I went on to describe what was involved and in general tried to impress him with what an important person I was about to become.

"How fast does the puck move?" he asked.

"Oh, sometimes over a hundred miles an hour," I answered with obvious pride.

"Well, Lloyd, you know that the human eye cannot accurately focus on an object moving at that speed?"

"I–it can't?"

What followed was an esoteric discussion of the limitations of human vision, a discussion which did more to intimidate than educate. Saccadic eye movement. Peripheral acuity. Concepts I didn't fully understand, but somehow sensed I would be experiencing in the future. I would later learn this was medical speak for Brett Hull's slap shot, a shot that comes in like a laser, hits the inside crossbar, and comes out again faster than can be seen with the naked eye. It also means Joe Sakic's amazingly quick release, a "now you see it, now you don't" trick frequently played simultaneously on goaltenders and goal judges alike. What I didn't know then is that I would later learn all about this medical fact the hard way . . . and on national television.

Not altogether certain I could do this, but mostly fearing I would be stuck back in the penalty box with Theoren, I awaited my professional debut. As a warm-up, I was assigned to do a preseason game pitting the Mighty Ducks against the New York Islanders. Although not a televised game nor a full house, I still felt a bit of pregame jitters as I took my seat directly behind Ron Hextall.

Few players at any position have had as auspicious an entry into the National Hockey league as Ron Hextall. In his first year he was voted to the All-Rookie team, was a First Team All-Star, earned the Vezina Trophy as the league's best goaltender, and became one of only four players in the history

*The author, here in the goal judge's box at the Pond, learned a valuable lesson on his first night from goalie Ron Hextall.*

> **Losing sight of the puck is not the only problem for the goal judge.**

of the NHL to win the Conn Smythe Trophy as Stanley Cup MVP despite playing on the losing team. Any thought I had that Philadelphia traded him to the Islanders because he was washed up was quickly dispelled.

Early in the contest, the Islanders went on a power play, putting intense pressure on the Ducks in their own end. Finally getting possession, the Ducks shot the puck all the way down the boards and went for a much-needed line change. A strong skater, Hextall raced to the boards, corralled the puck, and fired it back up ice to one of his teammates waiting at the blue line. Unfortunately, it caromed off that player's stick right onto that of an onrushing Duck who one-timed it at the now empty Islander net. Thinking it humanly impossible for anyone to stop the shot, I moved my thumb onto the goal light button. Just as I began to push it, I saw the thick blade of a goalie stick come into view and deflect the puck wide of the net.

Hextall, seeing the play develop, had taken two giant strides back towards the net, then dove, stretching out his stick and his 6' 3" body to its fullest to deflect the puck out of midair into the corner. This still ranks as one of the most dazzling saves I have ever seen before or since. Even though I was relieved not to have actually pushed the goal light button, I was terrified to think how close I had come to doing so.

In retrospect, I learned a valuable lesson that day from Ron Hextall. Never underestimate the ability of this caliber of player to pull off the seemingly impossible, to make the miracle play. I firmly believe that the players in the National Hockey League are the finest ice hockey players in the world, and any player who makes it to the NHL, whether for the Stanley Cup or the proverbial "cup of coffee," automatically puts himself into the highest competitive echelon of the sport.

I also learned that the job was a whole lot tougher than I thought. For one thing, you do not watch the game. You stay absolutely focused on the puck. When you can see it, that is.

During power plays, it seems every player on the ice jockeys for position in the slot directly in front of the goalie just as the defenseman lets a blast go from the point. With no chance to see it coming, the only option is to stare at the back of the net and pray. As entertaining to the fans as it is, when Gretzky sets up "in his office" behind the net, it plays havoc on the goal judge. Trying to follow his moves from that position is harder for the goal judge than it is for the other team's defensemen. Keeping the puck in view gets even harder when a giant like Jeff Beukeboom insists on starting his breakout plays by leaning against the glass directly in front of the goal judge's box.

Losing sight of the puck is not the only problem for the goal judge. Sometimes you see the puck, but your eyes play tricks on you. Like when it hits the outside of the net, causing the netting to fly, and your thumb to twitch. That's when it's prudent to follow the goal judge's motto, "better a second late, than a second early." The worst trick of all, however, is when the puck goes through the net. Yes, completely through the net. Even though the linesmen carefully check the netting before the start of each period of play, there have been instances when the puck is shot so hard it either finds or creates a weak spot in the netting. The goal judge is sure it came right at the net, but there it is, still in play. It happens so quickly, even the players are unsure about it.

As you can probably guess, the goalie doesn't volunteer to straighten matters out. There have been two such goals at the Ducks home rink, both of which happened so fast, they could only be decided by the video goal judge, who sits with his assistants and five cameras in a booth high above the ice surface. For him, these events are exciting, justifying his very existence. For the goal judge, they are the stuff nervous breakdowns are made of.

Fortunately, none of these problems presented themselves, and I finished up the Islander game without any difficulty. Next up for me was a regular season game against the Los Angeles Kings and the Great One. I could only imagine how exciting it would be to light up one of his goals. As it turned out, he was the one who got excited when I lit up a goal, but it wasn't quite for the reason I had hoped.

# Optical Delusion

## "There Is No Goal. Repeat. No Goal."

The Los Angeles Kings had their best season ever when Wayne Gretzky led a spirited run to the final round of the 1992–93 playoffs. Only a sharp curve and the need of a little Coffey derailed them within reach of the Stanley Cup. As the 1993–94 season began, the Kings and their fans looked forward to even greater success. By comparison, the Mighty Ducks of Anaheim were an expansion team in their first season of play. What they didn't have was a proven track record or marquee players. What they did have was a first-year head coach with a ferocious will to win and a ragtag band of players who couldn't stand to lose.

When these two teams met on December 26, 1993, surprisingly tied in the standings, there was more at stake than the two points for winning the game. There was also the matter of bragging rights for these teams who shared the same territory, but not the same press. The Kings were usually on the front of the sports page, while the Ducks were still considered part of the cartoon section. The Ducks saw this game as an opportunity to prove they could play in the same league with their close neighbors, and there would be a big audience to see this firsthand. The game was not only a sellout, but would be televised locally, nationally, and on cable. In short, it would be carried on every communications system known to modern man, with the possible exception of the Home Shopping Network and radio-free Europe.

When Supervisor Tony Guanci told me I would be working as a Goal Judge for this game, I couldn't help but feel a sense of pride in his confidence in me. Of course, the fact that one of the regular goal judges, Bill Bedsworth, was unavailable that night, probably had a little something to do with it, but I still regarded this as an honor I had earned. Since that first preseason game against the Islanders, I had worked as a goal judge in several regular season games without a problem. Dr. Terry's ominous lecture on saccadic eye movement had become a distant, fading memory. This was going to be a night I would always remember. Who knows, I might even get a little TV time out of this. As I would soon find out, I was going to get a lot more TV time than I anticipated or wanted.

As predicted, the game was played with tremendous intensity. Working behind the home net, I had to turn the red light on for three Kings goals, but the Ducks stayed in the hunt with two of their own. With the teams switching ends for the second period, Kelly Hrudey set up to defend the goal in front of me. For most of the period the teams battled up and down the ice, neither one having a good scoring chance. Then it happened. Intercepting an errant Kings' pass, Joe Sacco stepped over the blue line and fired a booming shot right on the ice and right on the net. Coasting out to cut off the angle, Hrudey made a big sweeping move with his stick to deflect it into the corner . . . and missed. Momentarily miscued by Hrudey's motion, I relocated the puck just in time to see it enter the net at full speed, and immediately come back out.

Certain the puck had crossed the goal line, hit the white bumper on the inside of the net, and gone back out, I turned on the goal light. As soon as I had done so, I had second thoughts. How did the puck get back into play so fast? Being basically in a soundproof box, I couldn't have heard it ring

*Did he or didn't he? The author thought Joe Sacco scored, but no one else did.*

> **It's hard to argue whether or not a goal has been scored with the person who has seen more of them than anyone on planet earth.**

off the goal post even if it had. I replayed it in my mind, and again concluded it had fully crossed the goal line. Seeing the red light go on had caused the fans to let out a thunderous cheer, but the players, Ducks included, continued to play as if nothing had happened. Even the incredibly loud and obnoxious horn that automatically sounds every time a Ducks goal is scored remained silent. Finally, one of the linesman, Brad Lazarowich, grabbed the referee as he skated out of the zone and pointed to the rotating red light above me. At the same time as the referee blew the whistle to stop play, the phone in my box rang. Being a direct hookup to the scorer's table, I knew it was going to be Guanci wanting to know what was going on. Well, actually, he wanted to know what the hell was going on. Each time I tried to explain what I saw, he would ask, "Then why is the puck out at center ice?"

Good question. It was probably the same one Gretzky was now asking me. There he stood, the Hockey God, right smack in front of me, his head shaking as if to say "no way," and his lips moving as if to say something about my ancestry. It's hard to argue whether or not a goal has been scored with the person who has seen more of them than anyone on the planet earth.

To make matters worse, which at the time seemed impossible, I was now being shown live on the Jumbotron pleading my case on the phone to Tony. There I was, gesturing frantically as if he would be more persuaded by body language than the English language. My humiliation was complete when the public address blared out,

"There is no goal. Repeat. No goal. The puck never crossed the goal line."

What a nightmare. My moment in the sun had turned into what seemed like hours of anguish in front of 17,174 fans. And it only got worse when I had to leave the goal judge's box between periods. As I walked up the steps to the main concourse, I was asked repeatedly by fans to explain exactly what happened on the "Phantom Goal." But as hard as I tried, no one seemed to understand or accept my explanation any more than Tony Guanci did.

Eventually, the game ended, allowing me to go home and spend a sleepless night replaying the whole scene: Hrudey fanning, Tony calling, Gretzky complaining. And through it all, me looking real stupid . . . on the Jumbotron, no less.

The next morning, I got up early and vowed to put the entire ordeal out of my mind. What's done is done. Even though I couldn't think of how, I consoled myself by thinking things could have been worse. Besides, I had a busy day that day. A bantam team I was coaching had qualified for the state championships, and we had a practice scheduled that morning. Skating onto the ice, I realized how much fun it is to be with these kids, a great group of hockey players whose love of the game exceeded even my own. But before I could even get the first drill under way, one of the players skated over to me and said, "Hey, coach. My parents are visiting friends back in Harrisburg, Pennsylvania, and they called to say they saw you on television last night."

Oh, no. In all the emotion, I had forgotten the game was being broadcast everywhere there was electricity. The only time they would have seen me was when I turned on a light that should have stayed off. I started to painfully realize I hadn't blown the call in front of only 17,174, I blew it in front of the world. With a push of a button, I had become internationally infamous. I began to consider entering the Federal Witness Protection Program—my only alternative to a life of shame.

A couple of years have passed since that fateful December night, and I have been a goal judge in almost a hundred games since then. Although I still wince when some fan laughingly asks me to explain that "Phantom Goal" again, I've pretty much gotten over being upset or bitter about blowing that call. And I never really did think seriously about joining the Federal Witness Protection Program. The way I figured it, with my luck, they'd probably send me to someplace where everyone already knows me.

Like Harrisburg, Pennsylvania.

# Away Games

## A Phone Booth View for the Playoffs

"We need to work hard to get into the playoffs. It's going to come down to the last few games. Every game is important. We need to bear down for every goal."

While that's probably what Coach Ron Wilson was saying to the Mighty Ducks players, it was certainly what the goal judges were telling themselves. The Stanley Cup playoffs are the Holy Grail for goal judges as well as for the players. The National Hockey League rules require that neutral site Off-Ice Officials be used during the playoffs, and we knew we would eventually be evaluated for such an assignment. We just didn't know when.

As I took my seat in the goal judge's box behind the home net on April 3, 1996, I was aware that this game would be a closely fought contest between two divisional rivals both battling for the final playoff spot. While each team had sharpshooters, they had gotten to this point on good goaltending.

The Edmonton Oilers, needing to get back into the playoffs, would start Joaquin Gage, a big goalie whose talent got him up from the minors in Cape Breton, and whose performance in the bigs would hopefully keep him from going back down. The obvious choice in net for the Ducks was Guy Hebert, whose second half performance was one of the main reasons they were poised for their first postseason play. They would play that night to a packed house. What neither the other goal judge working that night, Bill Bedsworth, nor I knew at the time was that among the cheering fans was Wally Harris, National Hockey League Supervisor of Officials. He wasn't there for entertainment; he was there on business.

The game lived up to its billing, and then some. Each goalie made incredible save after incredible save. One shot was trickling over the goal line when Ducks defenseman Bobby Dollas snatched it out with his stick before it crossed completely into red light territory. On another shot the puck rolled on its edge from post to post, right on, but not over, the goal line. Referee Dan Marouelli and I gave each other the thumbs up sign after the video goal judge backed up our "no goal" call. Bedsworth was being put to the test, too, as first Gage, then Hebert made miraculous saves in front of him. It was a game so brilliantly played by both goaltenders, it was a shame for either one to lose. It turned out to be Gage on the short end as the Ducks pulled out a narrow 1–0 win to keep their playoff hopes alive. Two weeks later, time ran out on the Ducks. Sadly, they would have plenty of it to prepare for the next season.

Our own playoff hopes got a boost when word was sent down to us after the game that we had done an excellent job. "Clear your calendar, we're going to Denver."

Guanci's words were music to my ears. He would be traveling as the Official Game Scorer, and Bedsworth and I would be the two Goal Judges. What a great duo to go on the road with. Tony, with his amazing stories dating back to when he managed the rock band Boston, and "Beds," a State Appellate Court Justice with an unparalleled sense of humor, would be great company.

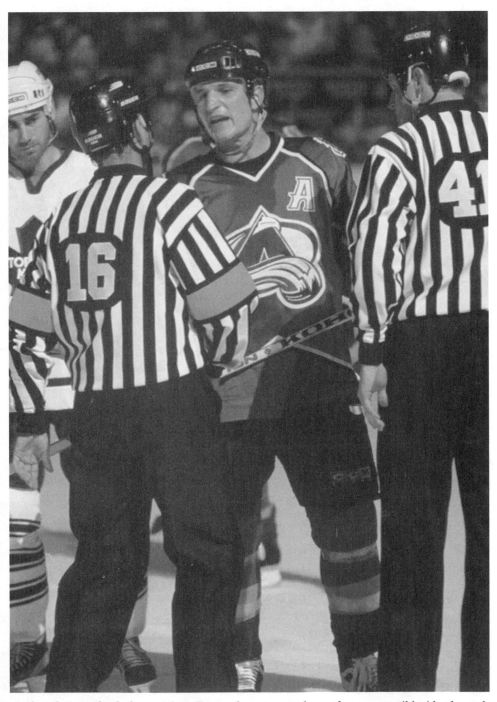

*A thunderous check from Adam Foote almost sent the author on a wild ride through McNichols Arena.*

> I came to town in a plane. I sure didn't want to leave it on a rail.

And what a great city to go on the road to. Denver has done a remarkable job at building a beautiful, user-friendly city equal in every way to my other favorite, Vancouver, British Columbia. Forget Paradise, I'd rather do time in either of these. We had portions of four days to spend in Denver, and much to see in our spare time, but business came first. After settling into our separate rooms, we decided to go check out the Avalanche home rink, McNichols Sports Arena.

Let's just say McNichols has the charm of one of the older National Hockey League sites. Obviously lacking the modern amenities of the Arrowhead Pond of Anaheim, McNichols has a certain quaintness about it. It also has 16,061 seats that are filled with knowledgeable fans who love their Avs. Narrow, somewhat uncomfortable seats, that's true. But when you jump up to cheer every hometown goal this team scores, you don't spend much time in them anyway.

Once in the arena, the first priority for Beds and I was to check out our respective goal boxes. National Hockey League Rule 37 (b) states that the goal judges shall be stationed behind the goals during the game, "in properly protected areas, if possible, so there can be no interference with their activities." It was always a source of great curiosity to me that protection of the goal judge would even be an issue. Protection from what. The players? Their shots? The fans. Were there incidents of attacks on goal judges that had been hushed up? And if the goal judge needed some type of protection, why should it only be provided if possible? Reading this rule always brought to mind that scene near the end of the original Frankenstein movie. You know, the one where the townspeople are chasing him around with lighted torches and bats in their hands. Maybe this is what would happen to me if I was to light up another "Phantom Goal."

Checking out these goal boxes was becoming extremely important to me. I came to town in a plane. I sure didn't want to leave it on a rail.

We walked over to the visitor's goal where Bill would be working in game one. What we saw when we got there was a goal box that could only be used in a Pee Wee game by a Pee Wee goal judge. A small door in the back provided entry into the pantry-sized interior, barren except for a backless bar stool and an on/off switch crudely anchored to the inside of the dasher boards. This thing was so small, it would be hard to think in it, let alone move.

I couldn't keep myself from laughing while watching Bill try gamely to squeeze in and out of it. Even though we assumed the other goal box would be the same, we decided to head over to the other end, Bill looking a little worse for wear after his struggles almost in and gladly out of the pint-sized box.

As we walked around the end boards I made a startling discovery. "Hey, where's the goal box?"

There we stood open-mouthed looking at the place where a goal box should be, but wasn't.

"It's in the back here. Come on, I'll show you," an attendant volunteered, and off we went, down a long cement corridor and around to the right where the Zambonis were resting.

"You see, the Zamboni doors are right behind the goal, so we rigged up this one on wheels."

The goal box wasn't a box at all. It could only be described as a popcorn machine on wheels, complete with large red and green lights mounted on top. The big smile on Bedsworth's face told me his every dream of revenge had just come true.

"You get in it through here," gesturing to a tiny rear door, "then once you're in, we close it up, and wheel it up to the glass." He neglected to tell me where I would sit, probably thinking I looked just smart enough to figure out someone would shove a stool in behind me right before they locked me in.

"Where do I sit?"

"We shove a stool in behind you right before we lock you in," he answered in a somewhat exasperated tone.

"Oh."

"Does he get out between periods, or does he stay in there until the game is over?" That was Bedsworth's question, but he was laughing so hard when he asked it, our tour guide didn't answer it.

"Well, do I?" I'm sure I impressed this guy a lot.

As we left the arena to go prepare for the game, I noticed Beds was walking with a noticeably jaunty step. And he was whistling. I, on the other hand, was still wondering whether or not I would be let out of that contraption between periods.

Exactly five minutes before game time, I stepped gingerly into what may be the only street-legal goal box used in the National Hockey League. After the introductions and National Anthem were completed, I was rolled into position, snug to the boards, and ready to work my first ever Stanley Cup playoff game.

In front of me were the Colorado Avalanche and the Chicago Blackhawks ready to do battle in the Western Conference semifinals. Within a few minutes of the opening face-off, 200-plus pound Adam Foote ran 200-plus pound Jim Cummins full speed directly into the boards in front of me. The force of the check jolted my portable goal box, which began slowly but surely to roll backwards. Fearful I would continue rolling completely out of the rink, I frantically searched in vain for the brake. I could only hope no one in Harrisburg, Pennsylvania was watching.

**I stepped gingerly into what may be the only street-legal goal box used in the National Hockey League.**

Suddenly, I accelerated back up to the boards and stopped exactly in my previous position, thanks to the timely intervention of the rink attendants. As I straightened back up, I could see Bedsworth all the way down at the other end. He looked like those big jars in science class, the ones where there's an animal stuffed in it floating in formaldehyde, its face flattened against the glass. Even though I was certain he was very uncomfortable in that wee little goal box, I was surprised to see he had such a big grin on his face. He would have even more to smile at as the game progressed. Like the time I dropped the switch for the goal light, nearly causing a stoppage of play as I reached to the floor with my chin hooked on the dasher board.

My biggest thrill came at the end of each period. It is extremely critical that a goal judge remain focused during the last seconds of each period, because when the scoreboard gets to zero, the green light above the goal box automatically comes on and simultaneously prevents the red goal light from being activated. Even though a goal is scored with time still on the clock, failure to light the light before it expires could lead to big problems, and in my case, more fodder for the folks watching in Harrisburg.

With this in mind, and being a playoff game and all, I was concentrating my hardest when time expired in the first period. In McNichols Sports Arena, when time expires and the green light comes on, something else happens. In a hurry to get the Zamboni doors open, which are also used by the Avalanche players to exit the ice, attendants immediately spin the portable goal box around, and race it back away from the boards. One second you're focused on the back of the net, the next you're being launched into orbit. My whole life and 16,061 fans passed before me repeatedly as I spun dizzily away down the corridor. Bill had himself a good old time watching that move.

Jeremy Roenick put an overtime power play goal in Bill's net to win Game One for Chicago, creating a challenge for Colorado in Game Two. Required by the National Hockey League rules not to work the same goal in consecutive games, the challenge for me was to fit in Bill's box for the next game. And I was going to do it if I had to spend the entire next day in the hotel sauna.

Arriving at McNichols for Game Two, Bill suggested we go down and check out our boxes, starting with the one I would be in. Nothing like loosening up with a few laughs watching me squeeze into the goal closet. As we turned the corner, we stopped dead in our tracks.

"We thought you'd like a little more room."

There stood one of the female ushers, holding open the side door to the most sumptuous goal box ever made. From where I stood, I could see a large stuffed chair inside with a small end table nearby to hold my favorite beverage. Bill was in shock. I couldn't resist.

"You see, Bill, the fine people here at McNichols understand that I have become accustomed to a certain level of treatment, and wishing to meet my every need, they have seen fit to provide this luxurious goal judging cabana. Hold on while I check this chair to make sure it's properly adjusted to my exact requirements."

I cannot tell you how great that felt, especially when I saw the rather disheartened look on his face. Now I would get to sit in opulence and watch Bill go off-roading at the other end of the rink. I stepped into the box and closed the door, smiling broadly as I watched Bill gnash his teeth. I settled in and gazed out onto the expanse of ice.

"Hey, where's the goal?"

"It's right over there, on your right," she answered.

Sure enough, there was the net, approximately six feet to the right of the goal box. I leaped out of the box in a panic.

"This can't stay here. I've got to be right behind the net." Instinctively, I began pushing, as if I could actually slide it into position.

"It won't move, silly. It's nailed down tight. They had to put it there because of the TV cameras."

I was stunned. Here was the Taj Mahal of goal boxes, and I needed a periscope to see the net. For a moment I thought I could actually hear TV sets being clicked on all over Pennsylvania.

"Good luck tonight," Bill cheerfully called over his shoulder. I'll bet he whistled all the way to the other side of the rink, too. Now it was my turn to spend the game with my face shoved up against the glass.

The game was played at a typical playoff level of intensity until a fan threw a not-too-fresh trout onto the ice. When the Public Address Announcer asked people not to throw foreign objects onto the ice, someone yelled back, "That's not foreign. We catch 'em locally."

Not wanting to delay the game any further, the linesman scooped it up, and tossed it into the penalty box. A short time later, Steve Smith of the Blackhawks ended up in the box, and almost immediately complained about the smell.

"We'll get it out of here at the break."

"I can't wait for the break. I want it out now," and with that Steve picked up the fish, and attempted to shove it through the much smaller hole in the glass separating the scorer's table from the penalty box. By the time the fish was finally through it, it was all but filleted. Fortunately the period ended allowing the hazardous waste team to clean up the mess.

Game Two was won by the Avalanche to even up the series. The teams headed to Chicago for Games Three and Four. We would be heading home with the hope that we might have a chance to do another playoff series. That would depend on a number of things beyond our control, but if the opportunity should arise, and it would require us to return to McNichols Sports Arena, I'm not taking any chances. I'm bringing my own goal box with me.

# The Phantom Strikes Again

## A Legitimate Goal?

The highlight of my work with the National Hockey League was doing the series at Colorado. In the first game, the Avalanche had several breakaways and close-in shots that Chicago goalie Ed Belfour had stopped in all-star fashion. And Patrick Roy was, well, Patrick Roy, rightfully considered the best clutch goalie in the game. Game Two was more of the same. Fittingly, both teams came out winners in that Colorado encounter. Watching these guys up close during crunch time was a thrill beyond description. There was only one way to top it.

"We've been picked to do Game Five of the Stanley Cup Final." I kept re-running Tony's message on my voice mail. Going back to McNichols Sports Arena was just fine with me. And I wasn't a bit worried about those goofy goal boxes. To do a final game, I'd sit there without any glass in front of me.

I started packing immediately. My reasoning was simple. No way Colorado could win in four straight. First of all, they would be playing the Florida Panthers, a team in only its third year of existence, but with a cast of characters—from the coach on down—for whom losing was not an option. Getting to the Final had been a test of skill, stamina, and courage

**"We've been picked to do Game Five of the Stanley Cup Final."**

against Boston, Philadelphia, and Pittsburgh. At the start of each of those series, the so-called experts predicted Florida would be blown out. The experienced Bruins fell in five games. The Flyers tried to beat them out of the playoffs, but lost in six. It took the Panthers seven games to finally oust the Penguins, who were favored to win with the scoring of Mario, Jaromir, and company.

Secondly, the Panthers had a goalie who liked crunch time as much as Patrick Roy. And John Vanbiesbrouck was out to prove he was the better of the two. Tied with Roy in goals against average at the end of regular season play, the Beezer was undoubtedly looking forward to a showdown.

And last, but far from least, the Panthers had acquired my personal choice for league MVP, Ray Sheppard. If he could save me from Probert, he could do anything. Yeah, packing the suitcase was the right move. Even if Florida didn't win the series, for sure they'd win at least one game. As the Finals progressed, I continued to feel Florida would at least win one game. Down one, two, then three games, my confidence never wavered. I kept the suitcase right by the door. I was going to Denver for Game Five.

The night of Game Four, I set up in front of the TV, volume cranked and munchies at the ready, and waited for the Panther victory. Just to make me sweat, they went into overtime. They were probably just toying with me like one of those cute little rats they kept throwing at each other. During a break in the action, I called Bedsworth on the phone.

"Pretty exciting, huh?"

"I'm not watching it."

"Waddya mean not watching it?" I couldn't believe I just heard that.

*One of the greatest playoff goalies ever, Patrick Roy was the winner in a Stanley Cup game no one deserved to lose.*

"I can't stand the suspense. I'm watching the 'History of Country Music' on cable." Bill was obviously cracking under the pressure of facing those teeny weeny goal boxes again.

On it went, into the next overtime and beyond. Roy and Vanbiesbrouck were obviously locked in some kind of do-or-die struggle. Then it happened. This big guy Krupp fires one through a crowd, and the red light comes on, just like it went in. No way! That goal judge must not know anything about saccadic eye movement or peripheral acuity. I kept waiting for his face to go up on the Jumbotron, but it never happened. They just showed Colorado running around with the Cup like the game was over.

Well, my suitcase is still packed, and sitting right by the door. Sooner or later, we'll all be going back to Denver. Because that was a "phantom goal" if there ever was one.

And believe me, I'm an expert on those.

# Picture This

## Q: What Does a Bottle of Beer and a Goal Judge Have in Common?
## A: Nothing Above the Neck

There are several perks to being a National Hockey League Off-Ice Official. One, of course, is being able to sit in the penalty box, close to players whose uniforms smell so badly it makes your eyes water. Another is to be locked in a confined area between two big angry men who yell threats of great bodily injury to each other, both with the present ability to carry them out. As wonderful as these perks are, they pale in comparison to the most significant perk of all: "picture time."

When I'm working the penalty box, the television cameras usually follow the miscreants into the bin hoping to get none too rare, but entertaining footage of grown men in the act of going berserk. And I'm usually right in the middle of it. Granted, I'm terrified, but there I am, nevertheless, handing the penalized player his equipment, making notes of the penalty on a clipboard, or just plain mugging for the camera. Warhol may have been right when he said we all may be limited to fifteen minutes of fame, but mine come in two minute increments, so I have to make the most of them. Though dozens of my friends say they've actually seen me on television, these are only fleeting glances that quickly disappear.

But working as a goal judge behind the nets is a chance to achieve the

> There I sit, directly behind the goalie, right smack in the middle of the action, a Kodak moment waiting to happen.

ego's holy grail: the printed picture. Cameras of photographers for the print media and those under contract to various studios or card companies are typically trained on the area of the nets, poised to record that split second moment in time of a great goal or save. And there I sit, directly behind the goalie, right smack in the middle of the action, a Kodak moment waiting to happen.

The following morning after working a home game as a goal judge, I run out to get the morning paper and immediately turn to the sports page. I look through the entire section hoping to see a shot of me, and when I find one, it's ego time. There I am, sitting on the edge of the seat leaning down to get the best possible view of the play, my nose nearly touching the glass, light switch clutched in my hand, frozen in time for all readers to see and looking as professional as can be.

With one slight exception: No head! That's right, the head is literally nowhere to be seen. For some strange reason which has never been fully explained to my satisfaction, sports photographers concentrate on the action, then perform identity surgery which they call "cropping." And one of the first things to fall to the cutting room floor is my head, my very persona. Since I'm not an important part of the action, as they see it, my head is just not necessary. They've made me the Ichabod Crane of hockey officials.

We Off-Ice Officials toil in relative anonymity as it is. Many fans are not quite sure of exactly what we do. Once when one of the goal judges was exiting his box at the end of the period he was stopped by a fan. Pointing at the video camera mounted on the top of the box, the fan asked if the goal judge's job was to operate the camera. When told that the camera was remotely controlled outside the rink in the network's truck, the fan paused and said, "So, your job then is to sit inside the box and protect the camera." Some of these California fans need a lot of education about hockey.

Thankfully, I always wear the Official Tie provided by the National Hockey League. Considered garish and styleless by most, it sticks out like a sore thumb and is roughly the same color. It has become the universal point of the cropping, right at the knot of the tie. That tie has been photographed more times than most celebrity faces. Without it, I'm just another faceless person. But once I put it on, I'm suddenly somebody. Well, at least something. I'm the headless goal judge.

There seem to be only two solutions to this very personal dilemma, this bar to my celebrity. One is to convince the league to issue me a tie with

*Old timers say the Pond is haunted by a Headless Goal Judge, and if you look closely you can see his official NHL tie.*

my picture on it. The other is to remove the glass behind the goalie so that I can lean out into the rink right at the time pictures are being taken. Something tells me the first solution is the safer one, but I'll bet the second one would get me the ultimate perk, one only available to the superstars of the sport: my face on a puck.

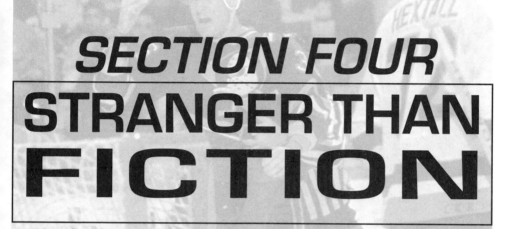

# SECTION FOUR
# STRANGER THAN
# FICTION

# Code of Honor

## The Misconduct Motto

The Lady Byng Trophy is awarded annually to the National Hockey League player who has exhibited, "the best type of sportsmanship and gentlemanly conduct." The list of previous winners includes some of the games most skillful and least penalized players. Players like Wayne Gretzky, Mike Bossy, and Marcel Dionne, to name a few. These are players whose skill attracted the rough stuff, but who managed to avoid it. Most of the time.

Basil McRae and Todd Ewen play a different kind of game. They are enforcers, ranking members of the goon squad who deal more in terms of punches landed than points scored. They don't give a cheap shot or a sucker punch. Their game is up front and in your face. Even though McRae is one of only ten players to score on a penalty shot in the history of the Stanley Cup playoffs, his game is less focused on offense than on being offensive. In his nineteen years with seven different teams in the National Hockey League, he's earned over 2,800 minutes in penalties. And counting. That's the equivalent of spending more than forty games in the penalty box. No slouch himself, Ewen has racked up over 1,900 penalty minutes in thirteen years playing for four different National Hockey League teams.

## But is there an honor code among these bad boys?

While other players practice such mundane skills as shooting and passing, enforcers perfect their ability to dish it out. Some have even taken martial arts instruction to assist them in changing the complexion of a game, usually to black and blue. Even hinting these players would qualify for the Lady Byng is enough provocation for mayhem. But is there an honor code among these bad boys? Is good sportsmanship a concept that is a part of their special kind of hockey?

On March 17, 1996, the St. Louis Blues and the Mighty Ducks met at the Pond on a night when Wayne Gretzky was making his return to southern California after The Second Trade. A capacity crowd was on hand to witness a duel between The Great One and The Next One, Paul Kariya. Somewhat predictably, the first duel was not between the superstars, but between the heavyweights.

Early in the game the puck was sent deep into the corner at the St. Louis end of the ice where a Blues defenseman attempted to freeze it against the boards. The pushing and shoving that ensued was originally intended to free the puck, but it soon deteriorated into a ten-player scrum. Within seconds two large figures began to drift out of the pack, facing each other with menacing looks. As the gloves and sticks were jettisoned, whistles blew, but to no avail. Ewen had latched on to McRae, and the territorial battle began. Although lasting only a relatively short time, Ewen was able to bloody McRae before the linesmen jumped in and separated them.

Once in the penalty box, McRae was adjusting his gear when he turned to Ewen, 20 feet away in the

**PENALTY BOX**

**Basil McRae**
Games Played: 654
Total Points: 148
**Penalty Minutes:** 2,806

home penalty box, and yelled, "Hey, nice going, taking me on when my shoulder's still out."

With a surprised tone in his voice, Ewen answered, "Wadda ya mean?" McRae went on to explain. "I've been out with a separated shoulder for two weeks. The only reason I'm playing tonight is we're short of guys."

In a genuinely apologetic tone of voice, Ewen said, "Hey, I'm really sorry. I didn't know about it or it wouldn't have happened."

Nothing more was said between the two nor did it have to be. Once the penalties had expired, Ewen returned to the ice and continued his aggressive play, as did McRae, even though hampered by the injured

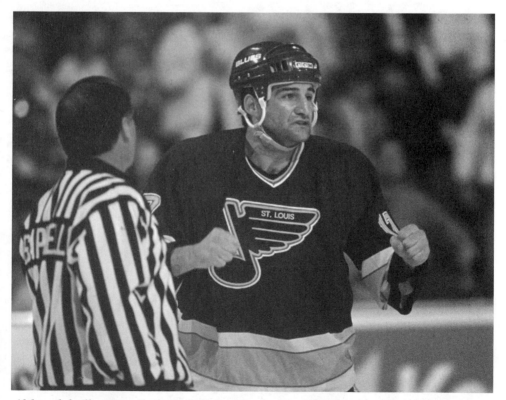

*Although he'll never win the Lady Byng Trophy, Basil McRae proves that even enforcers live by a code of honor.*

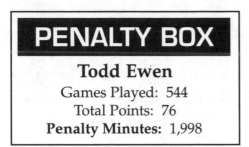

**PENALTY BOX**

**Todd Ewen**
Games Played: 544
Total Points: 76
**Penalty Minutes:** 1,998

shoulder. But for the remainder of the game the two kept their respectful distance from one another.

Although just moments before these two warriors had been nose to nose in a fierce battle, requiring both linesmen to risk life and limb to separate them, even the enforcers can occasionally "exhibit good sportsmanship and gentlemanly conduct." Lady Byng candidates? Probably not. But, good sports? Definitely!

# Knock, Knock, Who's There?

## It's a Hall of Famer!

William Scott "Scotty" Bowman is the winningest coach in the history of the National Hockey League, and there isn't a coach alive who wouldn't like to know how he does it.

The Mighty Ducks of Anaheim would sure like to know. From the opening night rout on, the Ducks have continued to have problems with Bowman's Detroit Red Wings. But then, so has every other team in the league. As an example, they set a National Hockey League record in 1995–96 for most wins in a season with 62. That made them a shoe-in for the Presidents' Trophy given annually to the team with the best regular season record. And they had won the same award the year before. Apparently, not having won the Stanley Cup in over forty years caused them to get a little confused during the playoffs each of those years, but they made up for it big time with their 1996–97 and 1997–98 Stanley Cup victories.

Their previous playoff problems were likely not the failings of their coach. Bowman is the only coach to take four different teams to the Stanley Cup Finals, and he's got more Stanley Cup rings than can fit on one hand to show he's a finisher. These are a few of the reasons he was

> Bowman fights for
> his team, just the way
> he expects them
> to fight for a win.

elected to the Hockey Hall of Fame in 1991, but they don't explain why he's so successful. I think I found out why.

The Ducks were taking another pounding from the Red Wings. Stevie Y was on a roll, but even more so was Sergei Fedorov, he of the intergalactic skates. Not only a Selke Award winning defensive forward, he was having a banner offensive year as well, then tied with the Great One for the scoring lead.

During the second period, Fedorov chased the puck into the Ducks end, arriving at the same time as Bill Holder. Just as Holder went to play the puck, Fedorov swooped in and lifted Bill's stick with his own. Trailing the play was forward Dino Ciccarelli, who spotted the puck loose at Holder's feet, pulled it out, and shot it in one motion. A groan went up from the crowd as the shot beat Hebert on the short side, falling in the net. Dino was being congratulated by his teammates as the announcement of his unassisted goal was made.

Detroit went on to win and, following the game, the Off-Ice Officials returned to their locker room in the basement of the Pond to complete the game forms. As we stood in the room, the door was suddenly thrown open, and storming through it was Scotty Bowman and his assistants.

"Why didn't you give Fedorov an assist on Ciccarelli's goal? That was bullcrap. You know he should have gotten one, why didn't you give it? Maybe you California people are just trying to help Gretzky win the scoring race or something."

The Supervisor patiently tried to explain that in the judgment of all the officials who reviewed the play, Fedorov, while making a great play, had never touched the puck himself. Scotty could not be appeased. Told he

*Red Wings coach Scotty Bowman stands up for his players the way he expects them to fight for a win.*

could send a tape to the League Office for review, he finally turned and stomped out of the room.

After he left, I realized I had just seen why Scotty has been so successful. He fights for his team, just the way he expects them to fight for a win. While I believe he was wrong about Fedorov getting an assist, he didn't hesitate to come and argue for what he thought was right. The Red Wings coach also showed why he's won the Jack Adams Award as the NHL Broadcasters' pick for best coach. In fact, about the only award he hasn't won is an Academy Award, and with performances like that, it won't be long before he has one of those, too.

# Goalie Dances

## Job Demanding Rituals

Prior to the start of every National Hockey League game, complex rituals unfold the moment the players skate onto the ice for the pregame warmups. Although these routines are performed repeatedly, they go largely unnoticed by all but the keenest observers. What may seem to be random skating, shooting, and stretching is in fact an extension of the Game Day Ritual that each player has honed to perfection over several years of playing hockey, and usually begins the moment each arises that morning, intensifying as the start of the game approaches.

Wayne Gretzky, for example, usually spends much of the warm-up period dodging players and their shots as he skates in a large circle between the blue line and the goal. Some players must make a certain shot into the net, such as hitting the crossbar, before they can go into the locker room prior to the start of the game. Others can only leave the ice after shooting a puck into the opponent's net. But the most unusual on-ice rituals clearly belong to the goalkeepers.

It has often been said that the most demanding job in sports is that of the goalie. If a team wins, it is usually the goal scorers who get the credit and the headlines. But if a team loses, the goalie is frequently faulted for failing to keep the puck out of the net.

Barring injury or collapse, the goalie is the only player on the ice for the entire game. Forwards and defensemen skate shifts of anywhere from 45 seconds to 2 minutes, but the goalie goes the whole sixty. Laden down with equipment that can weigh upwards of forty pounds, he waits in tense anticipation for that 100-mile-per-hour shot that requires a combination of superior eyesight, reflexes, and acrobatics to keep it from getting past him into the twine. Small wonder, then, that their rituals can be the most complex and repetitious.

Virtually all goaltenders perform continuous housekeeping chores around the nets. Sweeping the buildup of ice chips in a big arc from in front of the crease to the side of the net is a basic move. It not only acts as a release of tension, but tends to create a snow barrier to wrap-arounds or passes out to the slot. Additionally, most goalies continuously hydrate themselves with a water bottle kept handy on top of the goal. Various stretches and skating patterns in the vicinity of the net are also commonplace, and tend to vary little from one goalkeeper to the other.

However, some goalies have incorporated a few eccentricities into their rituals that take them a step beyond the others. Once he has the puck in his catcher, Bill Ranford will not allow the linesman to take it from him until he has flipped it into the air and it lands on the backside of the catcher. Aware of its importance to him, the officials will wait patiently until he is finished before they retrieve the puck.

Similarly, Trevor Kidd will never skate directly to his net, but will always skate first over the center ice face-off dot. As the Ducks' David Karpa found out, preventing Kidd from doing this by standing on the dot can bring about a very hostile reaction.

Then there are the ones whose ritualistic behavior is almost fetish-like, and so pervasive that nearly every move they make is part of a complex

*While most goalies have their own peculiar game day superstitions, Ron Tugnutt's rituals have evolved into an art form.*

> Nearly every move is designed to ward off goals and appease the Shutout Gods.

pattern designed to ward off goals and appease the Shutout Gods.

Ron Hextall goes through the pregame warm-ups like a man possessed. Taking his spot in the goal, he first skates through the crease from one side to the other, tapping his stick on the top right post, the center of the crossbar, and the top left post. Then he positions himself in front of the goal with his back to the net, and proceeds with his stick to beat out a rhythm on the pipes not unlike the one he beat out on Chris Chelios' head a few years back. When he's had enough practice, he skates at breakneck speed off the ice.

Once the game starts, the dancing doesn't stop. Hextall continues with all of the above, and adds checking first the straps on his right leg pad, then those on his left leg pad. Over and over again. But as repetitious as he is, Hextall doesn't hold a candle to the all-time champ.

Ron Tugnutt came to the Mighty Ducks of Anaheim by way of the Quebec Nordiques and the Edmonton Oilers, and he brought with him the most complicated ritual known to modern man. Having sat behind him on numerous occasions as a Goal Judge, I can tell you it's repeated *ad nauseum* throughout the game without a millimeter of variation.

Best described as a combination of figure skating, yoga, and Cirque du Soliel, it begins with a figure eight skate through the crease, and an abrupt turn up ice in a crouch to face directly wherever the puck is to be dropped. Coming to a stop twenty feet out from the crease, Tugger suddenly squats, then leaps straight up to a standing position. Without pause, he then rhythmically raps each leg pad with his stick, hops on one foot then the other, and tilts his head to the right as he lifts and touches his left foot. He's not done yet.

After a pause of about three seconds, he then raises his stick in his right hand up in the air and rubs the taped blade with the back of his catching glove. Had enough? He hasn't. Dropping into the classic goalie's stance he awaits the face-off. As soon as the puck is dropped, he accelerates backwards to the net, stopping abruptly each time with his shoulders only inches in front of the crossbar. The only thing he doesn't do is suck and spit water. Which is probably because, uniquely, he doesn't bring a water bottle with him onto the ice. And besides, he's too busy to drink water. He's almost too busy to stop shots.

I have this fantasy that right in the middle of this odd dance, someone comes in on a breakaway and slams on the brakes, waiting patiently until Tugnutt finishes before he resumes the rush. Or the guy fails to stop, fires the puck and scores, but the goal is disallowed because of a unique interpretation of the goalie interference rule.

I must admit I'm pretty skeptical about all this ritual business having any effect on the outcome of a performance. How could any intelligent person conclude that squats, leaps, raps, and rubs would bring good luck? Sounds like a bunch of hocus pocus to me. But I have noticed I've never misjudged a goal when I touch the top of the Goal Judge's booth with my right hand before stepping in first with my right foot, then my left.

Now that makes sense to me.

# Masked Men

## "In Your Face" Protection

After many years of thoughtful study, I have reached the following conclusion: at every level, goalies have traditionally gotten the short end of the stick. I remember how we got a goalie when I was a kid playing on the outdoor hockey rinks and ponds in Minnesota. The goalie was anyone who: a) didn't help shovel the snow off the ice; b) was a little kid, usually someone's younger brother or sister, who could actually be convinced that we wouldn't intentionally "lift" the puck when we shot it; or c) volunteered. There weren't many volunteers, and even fewer who volunteered more than once. But once we got them trussed up in all that bulky gear, it was too much trouble for them to quit, leaving us no choice but to fire away. Things weren't a whole lot better for the pros, especially in the early days of the National Hockey League.

Take any National Hockey League goalie from today, turn the clock back to the beginnings of the League, and he'd have more penalty minutes than Dave "Tiger" Williams. Hasek would be banned for life. The only way Eddie Belfour could get back into the rink would be with a ticket.

Imagine being a goalie prior to 1917, when it was a three minute penalty that had to be served by the goalie if he left a standing position. The term for this was "praying," which was probably exactly what they were doing. In those days, the goalies wore pretty much the same equipment as the players, which wasn't much.

It wasn't until four seasons later that the goalie was allowed to pass the puck without penalty. Imagine what would have happened to Billy Smith, Ron Hextall, or Chris Osgood when they not only passed the puck but scored with it. They better hope there's a hockey team at Alcatraz. The other option for a goaltender wasn't available either. Holding the puck without getting rid of it immediately was not only a penalty, but could be life-threatening. That's because that particular penalty called for a face-off from only ten feet directly in front of the net.

And don't ever do anything to cause a penalty shot. Originally, the shooter was required to shoot from a ten foot circle located 38 feet from the net. Apparently the goalies were successful in blocking some of these shots, so the rule was promptly changed to allow the shooter to "skate right into" the goalie before letting the shot go. And that's probably exactly what they did—skate right into the goalie. Remember, these were the guys with only rudimentary protective equipment. Leg pads were limited to only ten inches in width, and masks were non-existent. The story has oft been told of the struggle Jacques Plante went through before he was allowed to wear a protective mask in a game. This is a person who would go down in the history of the sport as one of its finest goalies, would be inducted into the Hockey Hall of Fame, but was publicly criticized for being too "chicken" to play the game because he felt the need to wear a mask.

To this day, Bobby Hull tells how he and his brother, Dennis, both with monster shots, would try to break a goalie's concentration by putting their first blasts head-high off the glass. After hearing a sound not unlike that of a shotgun, the netminder was usually thinking about things other than stopping the puck the next time one of the Hulls' shots aimed for the net.

*An elaborately decorated mask is a goaltender's personal statement, as Grant Fuhr and Mike Vernon can attest.*

> A goaltender's mask has become more than a piece of protective equipment, it has become his statement.

More than likely, he was thinking of major medical coverage and Last Will and Testament provisions rather than a shutout.

Things have gotten somewhat better for goalies now. "Crease crashing" has been minimized with the use of video replay, which can result in a goal being disallowed if an opposing player even thinks about being in the crease when the puck goes in. They used to refer to the steel goal posts as the netminder's best friend, but now it's a camera in a plastic box made by Sony or Panasonic.

And, thankfully, manufacturers are now producing a wide variety of protective equipment designed with the safety of the goalie in mind. This, of course, is good enough for everyone except Garth Snow, who prefers to get his goalie equipment at the local hardware store. Of all the equipment now available to goalies, the combination helmet/mask has made the most significant contribution to the health and longevity of goalies at all levels. For most, it has become more than a piece of protective equipment, it has become their statement.

With few exceptions, such as Detroit's Chris Osgood and Dominik Hasek of the Buffalo Sabres, nearly every goalie, from the National Hockey League on down to Pee Wees, wears a distinctively decorated mask, the front of which is typically adorned with team logos and wild color schemes. Costing as much as a thousand dollars, these masks are often more recognizable than the players who wear them. Young goalies not only copy them, they are even marketed in miniature, or as telephones and lamps.

The front of the mask may be devoted to the team, but the back of the mask is where you'll find the goalie's personal statement. Virtually every goalie in the National Hockey League has his moniker painted on the skull plate of the mask. Usually very subtle, in small print, it can be as simple as their name written in some stylistic way, such as: "Hebert" (Guy Hebert). Others get sort of folksy, like "Chevy" (Tim Cheveldae) or "Vernie" (Mike Vernon). A few just do the best with what they have to work with, like "Poops" (Daren Puppa). Jim Carey, now of the Boston Bruins, has tied his in with his Hollywood sound-alike's hit movie: "Ace."

But by far, the biggest "in your face" on the back of any mask is on the one worn by Grant Fuhr. He simply has five miniature Stanley Cups painted on there: a reminder of exactly how good he is.

# Goalie Save

## One for the Zebras

Mikhail Shtalenkov is big by goalie standards. Standing 6' 5" in skates and full goaltender regalia, he covers a whole lot of net. What little net can be seen is usually covered so quickly by a stick or glove that opponents must think they're shooting at mirages. And he's not afraid to leave the pipes to make the play, which he does with alarming frequency while chasing down dump-ins and rebounds. Although he's not as much a roamer as former Los Angeles Kings goalie Robb Stauber, who spent as much time at the hash marks as in the crease, Mikhail has proven he's just as capable handling the puck as he is at blocking it.

It was these skills that enabled him to lead the Unified Team to the gold medal at the 1992 Winter Olympics in Albertville, France. Along the way, he lost only one game while earning the lowest GAA (1.63) in the tournament. Clearly, growing up in Moscow and watching his idol, Vladislav Tretiak, play goal helped the big Russian (called Mike by his teammates) develop into a technically sound and highly competitive netminder.

Shtalenkov is not only big, he seems to be made of iron. Despite multiple pad stacks and dashes for the dump-in, he has never missed a game due to injury or illness in his first four seasons with the Mighty Ducks of

Anaheim. But in a game early in the 1996–97 season, that streak almost ended. The fact that it didn't may very well be the result of the quick thinking and intervention by the smallest guy on the ice that night.

Referee Kerry Fraser is not hard to spot out on the ice, and it's not because of the zebra stripes and bright orange armbands he wears. Most noticeable is that he seems way too small to be keeping the peace among professional sports' rowdiest performers. The tip-off that he is not intimidated by them is that he is one of the few On-Ice Officials who does not wear a helmet. And you absolutely can't help but notice he's not wearing a helmet: Kerry Fraser is not only the most perfectly coifed person to ever come out of Sarnia, Ontario, he may be the most perfectly coifed person on the planet. His hair is always immaculately combed, not a strand out of place. Even more remarkable is the fact that as he skates up and down the ice, minute after minute, period after period, it remains completely unruffled. Some are convinced he either has the world's best barber or he shampoos with plaster of paris.

He keeps the peace not with an iron fist, but with a firm demeanor and a photographic memory of the rule book, which he applies equally to both teams whether in the first period or the third. Witness the time he gave Tie Domi a double minor: two for roughing and two for unsportsmanlike conduct. Of course, Tie Domi considers a roughing penalty a compliment, but to get two for unsportsmanlike conduct was an insult that caused him to unleash a raucous barrage of expletives, his point apparently being "Okay, I punched somebody, but I was a good sport about it."

Kerry, halfway across the rink awaiting the ensuing face-off, ignored Domi for the first few seconds, assuming Tie would tire of his tirade and stop. But with the same stamina he has when he brawls, Domi continued on until finally the referee had heard enough. Turning directly towards him, Fraser fixed him with a stare that had ten minute misconduct written all over it.

*Referee Kerry Fraser helped keep goalie Mikhail Shtalenkov out of harm's way, and didn't even muss his hair doing it.*

> Shtalenkov is not only big, he seems to be made of iron.

Seeing that look, and knowing Fraser would do what he had to do to maintain control of the game, Domi paused, then quietly sat down. Make no mistake about it, Tie Domi fears no man, but he's not a fool. For more than twenty-three years as a referee in the National Hockey League, Kerry Fraser has earned a reputation as an official who will take whatever steps are appropriate to ensure a fair game. And apparently a safe one as well.

On this particular night, Shtalenkov was getting the chance to start in goal for the injured Guy Hebert. Always in great shape, and always ready to play, Mikhail was eager to defend against the visiting Ziggy Palffy and his New York Islander teammates. Although under 6' and less than 200 pounds, Palffy doesn't keep to the perimeter. With enough talent to stick handle through a picket fence, he goes straight to the crease before letting a shot go. Very often, he's followed there by his buddies, who are prepared to celebrate his goal or smack in a rebound of their own. When joined by the opponent's defenders, the predictable result is a frenzied scramble for control of the puck.

While goalies prior to the 1917–18 season, were given a three minute penalty for leaving their feet, modern goaltenders are proficient in "butterfly" and pad stacking techniques which bring them down closer to the action and closer to danger. As a result, goal mouth scrambles occur several times in each game, and while exciting for the fans, they can be hazardous to the players, particularly goalies. The near fatal injury to Clint Malarchuk is vivid testimony to the dangers of being too close to razor sharp skates moving at a high rate of speed in random directions.

Early in the second period, Palffy took a pass inside the Mighty Ducks zone and made a beeline to the net. Like water in a whirlpool, everyone on the ice seemed sucked toward Shtalenkov, who stood his ground until the last possible second. Dropping simultaneously with Palffy's release, he smothered the puck just in time to prevent a goal, but too late to stop the onrush.

In the ensuing goal mouth scramble, several players began to push and shove each other, their skates and sticks coming perilously close to the downed goalie. Realizing Shtalenkov's vulnerable position, Fraser darted to the net just in time to grab a player as he was about to fall on the goalie. As he did so, the off-balance player's stick came up and banged against the side of the referee's head with a thud audible to everyone on the ice. After the players had been separated and order eventually restored, one of the linesman skated over to Fraser and asked, "Do you think you'll need some ice for that, Kerry?" The concerned look on the linesman's face changed to a chuckle when Kerry answered, "No, but I may need some more hair spray."

That game ended in a tie, and Shtalenkov went on to complete another injury-free season. Being in great shape, playing smart, plus a measure of good luck can prevent most injuries to goalies. But sometimes it takes more than that to stay off the injured reserve list. Sometimes it takes a great save by the ref.

# Zebras

## The Workhorses of the NHL

I used to think that professional hockey players were the most durable of all athletes. Seemingly impervious to pain, they have been known to play through injuries that would have been season-enders for athletes in other sports. There is the classic story, for example, of one Andre "Moose" Dupont, then of the Philadelphia Flyers and in the midst of a career that would last thirteen years in the National Hockey League, between 1970–1983.

During those years the Flyers were known as the "Broad Street Bullies," a name they lived up to every game, including a few that got their names on the Stanley Cup two years in a row. The fans in Philly liked their hockey tough. What they didn't like was a somewhat slow defenseman, who several times during a game would see a player on the other team, first in front of him, then behind him, both times with the puck. The fans got on Moose pretty hard. It got so he could do no right, and every time he touched the puck, he'd hear the raspberries. Unfortunately, the fans didn't know what his teammates did: Moose had a pumper that more than made up for what he might lack in the legs. They were to understand this only after Dupont volunteered for some high speed dental work performed right before their very eyes.

During a late season game, Moose went down to block a first period
shot from the point, but mistimed it. Oh, he blocked the shot, all right, but
with his face and not his pads. Without a shield to stop or deflect it, the
puck hit him square in the mouth, extracting several of his teeth the hard
way. Moose got up from his pool of blood and molars, and skated immediately to the dressing room. Even his detractors would have understood
a week or two off, so you can imagine the reaction when he returned to
play—in the third period—of the same game. From that moment on,
Moose could do no wrong. Until the day he retired, he continued to be a
fan favorite on a team heavy with stars and future Hall of Famers.

There are many other stories of players who have shrugged off time in
sick bay to continue on the ice. But these are not the only athletes on the
ice. In fact, they might not even be the best-conditioned athletes out there.

Since having a rinkside seat courtesy of the National Hockey League,
I have developed a great appreciation for the stamina, skill, and even
courage of the On-Ice Officials. Not that these are traits of recent origin.
Like the Moose Dupont story, there are similar ones about the referees and
linesmen. Take John D'Amico, a Toronto native with experience as both a
linesman and referee in the National Hockey League. During a particularly rough series between Boston and Montreal, D'Amico had the difficult
job of trying to separate Stan Jonathon while he was busy putting an end
to Pierre Bouchard's career as an enforcer. In doing so, D'Amico caught an
accidental stick in the face from Terry O'Reilly, an accident worth fourteen
stitches. Undaunted, he can be seen in film of the incident pulling the
fighters apart, and continuing to minister to the needs of the injured
Bouchard despite bleeding profusely himself.

Scenarios like these continue to be acted out every game day on rinks
throughout the league, and while players get cheers and pay raises for it, the

Officials who skate with them do so largely in anonymity. Even their names on the back of their uniforms have been replaced recently by numbers.

Did I say skate with them? In reality, a player typically skates a shift lasting one to two minutes. Then goes to the bench for a breather, water, and a towel. Some players, such as Chris Chelios of the Blackhawks, may be on the ice for as many as thirty minutes of a sixty-minute game. But the Officials are out there for the whole game, which routinely lasts three hours or more. Every shift skated by the individual players is skated by the Officials.

Up and down the ice, stopping, accelerating, turning. All the while watching for infractions, and making split-second calls which are often disputed by one team or the other. Both the National Hockey League and

*On-Ice Officials, like the legendary John D'Amico, might be tougher than the players they're paid to watch over.*

> When a fight breaks out, the players go to their respective benches, but the linesmen go to the action.

the National Hockey League Officials Association have set high performance standards of conditioning, skating ability, and knowledge of the game rules and procedures, making this job one of the most demanding in sports.

When a fight breaks out, the players go to their respective benches, but the linesmen go to the action. More than a few have caught a stray punch or stick, some even intentional ones, when stepping between players intent on inflicting bodily injury on one another.

Wearing lightweight equipment to keep up with the action, they are often hit with shots and checks which cause injuries ranging from uncomfortable to agonizing. While working a Ducks game, Linesman Baron Parker was run into the boards with such force he was knocked unconscious, and had to leave the ice by stretcher and the arena by ambulance. While working a televised playoff game, Referee Mark Faucette lost two front teeth to an errant puck, but continued to officiate the game. Referee Rob Shick has been hit with a puck more times than most goaltenders.

Sometimes injuries can come in bunches. During one Ducks game, the puck had been frozen by the goalie, causing a face-off. The first linesman stepped in, dropped the puck, and was promptly cut on the forehead by one of the centers' sticks. After a brief delay for medical treatment, the other linesman stepped in for the new face-off, dropped the puck, and was promptly cut on the side of his head by the other center's stick. The referee ended up being the only healthy one left to complete the face-off.

I've concluded that making unpopular calls is the least of their worries. For them this is truly a dangerous occupation. I still have tremendous respect for the professional hockey player. But if you really want to see a superbly conditioned athlete with extraordinary stamina and skill, the next time you go to a hockey game take a look at the officials working it. You'll have plenty of opportunity to do so. They're out there the whole time.

# Fellow Travelers

## The Banger Shuffle

Warren Rychel is a well-traveled individual. He's played professional hockey in just about every city that has a team. His résumé reads like an atlas. Four teams in the Ontario Hockey League: Sudbury, Guelph, Ottawa, Kitchener. Four teams in the International Hockey League: Peoria, Saginaw, Indianapolis, Kalamazoo. Then throw in a stop at Moncton of the American Hockey League. Now you can add his five teams in the National Hockey League: Chicago, Los Angeles, Toronto, Colorado, and Anaheim. Fourteen cities in all. This guy has spent more time in the air than Lindbergh. When he answers the phone, he doesn't know whether to say "Hello" or ask "Where to?"

His résumé reveals a whole lot more about Warren than simply where he's been. It speaks volumes about his determination, his persistence, his commitment. Others might have called it quits long ago, but that word is not part of Rychel's vocabulary. Which is precisely why he's an excellent example of what coaches refer to as a "role player."

Every team in the National Hockey League needs star players, players with the ability to fill the net as well as the house. These are the players with the big headlines and the bigger contracts. But to be a contender, every team

**Every team needs a supporting cast, who get big bruises but little press.**

needs a supporting cast, a cast of role players who get big bruises but little press, and are often appreciated more in the locker room than in the stands. The only time you see these guys is when the spotlight happens to shine in the corners. And chances are good that if Rychel's on the ice that's where you'll find him, practicing more give than take to get the puck out to the point or the slot. Warren Rychel is a natural-born corner man. For one thing, he doesn't know the meaning of the word coast. If someone was to design a car after him, it wouldn't have a reverse gear or a brake pedal. And that's pretty much how he plays the game. All full ahead.

While he can score the odd goal, he knows these teams didn't pick him for his stickhandling. He's there to create opportunities for his teammates, and to cancel them for opponents. He does a good job at both of these. So good that he played a "major" role in helping the Los Angeles Kings to the Stanley Cup Finals in the 1992–93 season with a league-leading 30 major penalties. That same rugged style of play got his name on the Cup with the Colorado Avalanche in 1995–96.

The biggest measure of Warren Rychel's courage is his lack of size. At 6', 205 pounds, he's only a cruiser weight by National Hockey League standards, but he's fought every heavyweight in the league. In the 1993–94 season, he finished third in the league in total penalty minutes, behind only veteran peacemakers Tie Domi and Shane Churla.

Without a doubt, Mike Peluso is a heavyweight, all 6' 4" and 225 pounds of him. It's not just his size that's intimidating, it's the total package: long hair, square jaw, and a glowering stare that says "try me." Since literally breaking into the National Hockey League in the 1989–90 season with Chicago, he's made a career of the rough stuff. With over 1,800 minutes in the bin, he's given writer's cramp to every

*A journeyman peacemaker, Warren Rychel plays an important, if unglamorous, role for his team.*

Penalty Timekeeper in the League.

Working hard in the corners is second nature to a guy who was raised near the Mesabi Iron Range in Northern Minnesota. Rough stuff in the corners must seem like a vacation compared to the mining jobs of his able-bodied relatives. Watching them not only taught him the value of hard work, but was a great incentive to do well in professional hockey. Otherwise, the helmet he'd be wearing would have a light on it.

Having played for five different National Hockey League teams, Peluso is also a well-traveled guy. Ironically, on one of those teams, the Blackhawks, he was teammates with Warren Rychel. Now several seasons later, they were to meet again where they would greet each other the only way bangers can.

As the midseason game between the St. Louis Blues and the Mighty Ducks wore on, play steadily became more intense. Dump-ins were chased down at full speed with the hope of gaining possession down low. When Bobby Dollas put in a hard-around, Rychel knew right where to go, and so did Peluso. Peluso got there first, but Rychel never slowed, and the result was a bone-jarring collision. Any other players would have gone down, but the two former teammates only ended up face-to-face. Nothing needed to be said between these two whose respective roles on their teams made what happened next instinctive.

Even as the gloves were being dropped, blows were being thrown. The battle, though brief, was furious, with Peluso using his reach advantage to eventually score the win. A big cheer went up for Rychel by fans who knew that not backing down from a much bigger opponent was itself a victory. Once settled in the box, Peluso immediately turned to Rychel.

**PENALTY BOX**

**Warren Rychel**
Games Played: 436
Total Points: 95
**Penalty Minutes:** 1,466

"Hey, Rychs. I hear you and the Mrs. had a kid."

"Yeah, we did," Warren answered with a sheepish grin on his face. "They're in the stands tonight."

"Well, congratulations, man."

**PENALTY BOX**

**Mike Peluso**
Games Played: 520
Total Points: 97
**Penalty Minutes:** 2,058

Having gotten the pleasantries out of the way, Peluso could now ask the question that is uppermost in the minds of all role players.

"You been scoring any?" Rychel just shook his head.

The dream of every checker is scoring the game winner, of suddenly finding that elusive scoring touch that would get them ovations for points instead of punches. How great it would be. The endless high fives and backslaps from teammates, and the postgame press conference, where "the score" would have to be described over and over in minute detail. After all, talking about goals is almost as much fun as scoring them.

Alas, those opportunities come their way about as often as Halley's Comet. The press conferences and the long-winded descriptions are left to the stars, and the bangers toil in the relative obscurity of the corners. And maybe that's why even when they run into an old teammate, they fight. Maybe it's because there's not much to talk about.

# Say What?

## Learning the Game Is Easy; It's Understanding It That Takes Time

For much of the history of the National Hockey League, Canadian players dominated team rosters. Boasting what were then considered to be state-of-the-art training programs, facilities, and equipment, Canada was able to produce more than enough high quality hockey players to go around. As the sport expanded in numbers of professional teams and in international popularity, so too did the need for additional players, and in 1969, the first European-born player was taken in that year's entry draft. Mirroring the continued growth of the sport, countries other than Canada accounted for almost 42% of all players taken in the most recent Amatuer Entry Draft. European players coming to the National Hockey League face substantial cultural adjustments long before their first game, not the least of which is language.

Oleg Tverdovsky came to the Mighty Ducks of Anaheim as a shy nineteen year old from Donetsk, USSR, with maximum skills and minimum English. Drafted first by Anaheim, second overall in the 1994 entry draft, he was the kind of defenseman the Ducks were looking for: a gifted skater who liked to jump up into the play, with a strong shot and the accuracy to finish it.

> European players
> coming to the
> National Hockey League
> face substantial
> cultural adjustments
> long before their first
> game, not the least of
> which is language.

As could be expected, Oleg had some initial difficulty adjusting to the level of play in the National Hockey League. In an effort to speed up the process, Coach Ron Wilson paired him with team captain Randy Ladouceur, a veteran defenseman with fourteen years National Hockey League experience with three different teams. Considered a stay-at-home defenseman, it was hoped Randy could accelerate Oleg's learning curve and help him acquire the necessary skills to win himself a regular spot in the lineup. Randy took his mentor's role seriously, using every opportunity to instruct his pupil in the nuances of big league defense.

During a regular season game between the Ducks and San Jose, Randy was serving one of his rare penalties when he was joined by Tverdovsky, who had been caught out of position and in desperation had hooked an opposing player. No sooner did Oleg settle into the box than Ladouceur immediately began explaining the mistake he had just seen Oleg make. Complete with pointing and gesturing, Randy continued on for the duration of his penalty with his detailed explanation, often repeating important points several times to ensure he was getting his message across to the young Russian.

Although he remained staring straight ahead, Tverdovsky constantly nodded his head, signaling his comprehension of the finer points of this mini-seminar. His

## PENALTY BOX
**Randy Ladouceur**
Games Played: 970
Total Points: 164
**Penalty Minutes:** 1,381

*Not the most fluent of English speakers, Oleg Tverdovsky lets his stick do the talking for him.*

**PENALTY BOX**

**Oleg Tverdovsky**
Games Played: 265
Total Points: 125
**Penalty Minutes: 97**

penalty over, Ladouceur left the box with the satisfied look only a teacher can have when his student finally sees the light. As I closed the door to the box and turned towards Tverdovsky, he looked at me and said, "Why he say?"

*****

Fast forward to the second half of the 1995–96 season. The Winnipeg Jets are preparing for their move to Phoenix by lightening their load, and offer to trade All-Star Teemu Selanne. Yes, the same Teemu Selanne who set a still-standing record of goals (76) by a rookie. The Mighty Ducks pounce on the opportunity to acquire one of the sport's most gifted offensive stars, and give up Tverdovsky, Chad Kilger, and a draft pick to complete the deal.

Since his arrival in Anaheim, Selanne has exceeded even the lofty expectations of the management, his teammates, and the fans. He is the perfect compliment to Mighty Ducks star Paul Kariya. Both score at an amazing rate by combining skating speed, vision of the ice, shooting accuracy, and playmaking ability, while maintaining a "Lady Byng" temperament in the face of aggressive shadowing by opponents. As an added benefit to the image-conscious Disney, Teemu is not only a team leader, but a fan favorite who makes himself available for a variety of local charitable and fan appreciation activities.

While overjoyed to have obtained a star of the magnitude of Selanne, many Duck fans miss Oleg's end-to-end rushes, accomplished with blinding speed and magical moves. At least in a Ducks' uniform. Now they have to see him do it as a Coyote or in the All-Star game.

And although his English has gotten a lot better, he doesn't have to use it very much. With annual point totals nearly double what they were in Anaheim, it's obvious he's been letting his stick do most of the talking.

# Cheap Skate

## The Brothers Mironov

In the long history of the National Hockey League, there have been several well-known brother acts, such as Hull, Mahovlich, Richard, Stastny, Broten, Courtnall, Hatcher, and Hunter to name a few. For sheer numbers, none can match the six Sutter brothers, all of whom played in the National Hockey League at the same time. A few more siblings and they could have had their own franchise. Of course, the coaches of players like Yzerman and Modano wish they had twin brothers ready to follow them into the NHL. Alas, no such luck.

One set of brothers made the big step into the National Hockey League from long distance. Boris and Dmitri Mironov came all the way from Moscow, Russia, with limited English but exceptional hockey skills. Both play defense, both have big shots, and both can handle the puck with the skill of a surgeon.

Their hockey careers began when their father enrolled them as small boys in the Red Army Hockey School in Moscow. Progressing up through the ranks, each ended up playing for CSKA of the Russian elite league, although at different times. By then they had matured as hockey players and as men, both reaching 6' 3" and weighing right around 220.

Not only are they similar in size, they play the same style of game. Each is capable of scoring, usually by assisting on goals, and both spend about the same amount of time in the penalty box. And even though Boris is almost seven years younger than Dmitri, they almost look like twins. From where I sit, however, there is one subtle and intriguing difference between the two.

Boris Mironov wears the latest model ice skates, composed of high-tech materials, costing several hundred dollars per pair, and he probably replaces them each season with the same or a similar model. But not so for his brother. Dmitri, who could have any skates his feet desire, continues to wear one of the oldest model of skates made, the Bauer 92.

Players in the National Hockey League can have any piece of equipment they want as long as it's legal under the rules. Because they play in the most prominent league, equipment manufacturers and suppliers go to great lengths to "encourage" them to use, wear, or endorse their respective brands. In short, they get their pick of the best equipment made in the world. And of all the equipment they select, none is more important than the skates they wear.

While there are several manufacturers of quality ice skates, perhaps the best known is Bauer. Bauer is not only among the more famous brand names of hockey skates, but they are probably worn by more amateur and professional hockey players than any other. For example, I'm sure if an inventory was made of the skates worn by players in the National Hockey League, Bauer would come out way ahead of any other brand. Bauer's top-of-the-line model is the 5000 Comp Supreme. Before that, they offered the 4000 Supreme. Then the 3000 Supreme. That's right, their earlier big seller was the 2000 Supreme, which had replaced the Bauer 1000. So imagine how long ago a Bauer 92 was on the shelves. Probably sometime during the Eisenhower Administration.

*Whether it's frugality or superstition, Dmitri Mironov is in a league of his own when he laces up his skates.*

> Maybe he thinks the phrase "old-time hockey" refers to equipment.

For some reason, Dmitri prefers wearing skates that are now most often found in antique stores or at swap meets. It could be he continues to wear them because of the fit, but Bauer would certainly custom fit any model to the exact shape of a National Hockey League player's feet. Possibly it's because the model number 92 corresponds to the year Dmitri first played in the National Hockey League, but passing on lighter, firmer, ergonomically-correct equipment as important as skates seems too extreme a sacrifice simply for the sake of superstition. Maybe he thinks the phrase "old-time hockey" refers to equipment. But I think there is another more practical reason he chooses to wear skates that are ancient history to almost every other player in the NHL.

This could be a very clever move on Dmitri's part that will not only guarantee him a long career as an NHL player, but could also land him a front office job when his playing days are over. After all, he was saving Disney over three hundred dollars a year, and that's the spirit of economy they admire.

This could be a very risky move for the players, however. Once Disney realizes how much money there is to be saved in equipment purchases, the Ducks could become the only team in professional hockey to play their games in street clothes.

# Trade Talk

## Eenie, Meenie, Minie, Moe, a Scorer's Touch or a Brawler's Blow

There's a saying in hockey that natural goal scorers don't see the goalie, they see the net. If that's true, Teemu Selanne wouldn't know a National Hockey League goalie if he bumped into him. In his first year in the league, Teemu proved the part of the net he saw the most was the back, which he saw for a still-standing record 76 times. Teemu came to the National Hockey League after a career as a schoolteacher in his native Finland. Now he makes the big bucks schooling defensemen.

Selanne has learned that to produce for his team at the level they expect, he has to be in top physical condition. In every game he plays, Selanne is often the subject of intensive shadowing of the hands-on variety. At 6', 200 pounds, Selanne can take a hit and dish out his own in return. With that combination of skill and strength, Selanne's performance has been phenomenal, starting with a Calder Cup-winning freshman season for the Winnipeg Jets. Despite his superstar performance with the Jets, he was traded in his fourth season to Anaheim.

To close the deal on Selanne, the Mighty Ducks had to part with two excellent prospects, Oleg Tverdovsky and Chad Kilger. From the standpoint of offense, it's clear they made the right decision. In the first tw

> On many, many occasions during his time with the Mighty Ducks, Todd would predictably end up in the penalty box.

seasons since the trade, Selanne scored 67 goals compared to only 16 for Tverdovsky and Kilger combined. Most of those goals were highlight film specials, having been scored in every conceivable way: coast-to-coast, slapshots, wristers. One of them was even scored while he was flat on the ice.

Todd Ewen, on the other hand, is used to putting players flat on the ice, like his one-punch knockout of then-heavyweight champ Bob Probert. Teams acquire his services not to put up points, but to put down those players who dare to start the rough stuff. He has a role to play, and many feel that if not as important as an offensive star's role, it is nevertheless vital to the overall success of any team. Todd takes that role seriously. On many, many occasions during his time with the Mighty Ducks, Todd would predictably end up in the penalty box. And his time in the box was far from quiet time.

During the course of each penalty, Todd would concentrate totally on the play on the ice. He would act as cheerleader and critic by continually yelling encouragement or instruction to his teammates. It was obvious why he wore the "A" on his sweater. He knew his role was not only to play the game to the best of his ability, but to encourage his teammates to do the same. It was also obvious he enjoyed the role of being a team leader. But even more thrilling than turning someone's lights out is turning the red one on, especially when it rarely happens.

While sitting in the penalty box on one of his frequent visits, Todd Ewen, checker, watched as Teemu Selanne, scorer, picked up the puck in his own zone and went long distance weaving through heavy traffic to core one of his patented goals. It was the kind of play that brings fans to

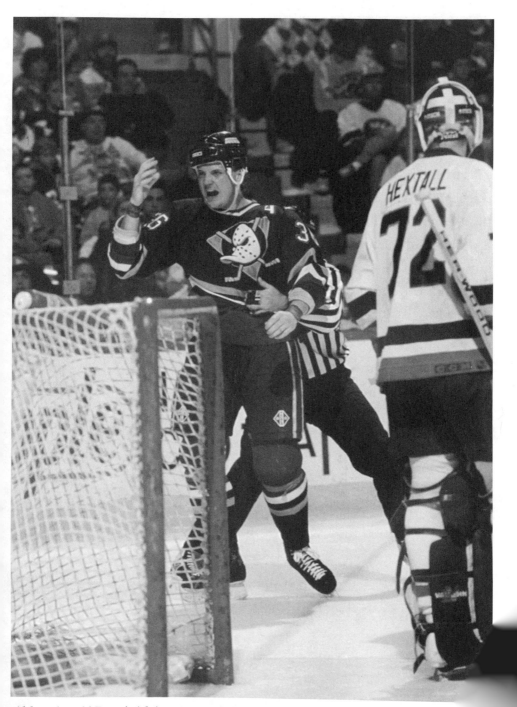

*Although Todd Ewen's job is to protect his more offensively-gifted teammates, he so*
*wishes he could trade his punches for points.*

**Todd Ewen**
Games Played: 544
Total Points: 76
**Penalty Minutes:** 1,998

their feet even if they're watching the game at home. Over the roar of the crowd, I heard Ewen let out a sigh and say, "What I wouldn't give to have hands like that for just five minutes."

For the first time it occurred to me it's not only the fans who admire the scorer's touch. Here was one of the sport's top cops, possessed of prodigious fighting skills, whose role has been, and always will be, to protect guys like Selanne. Todd's remarkable ability to do this has earned him not only respect throughout the league, but a very good living. Yet it's clear Todd would trade his skills in a minute for even a temporary loan of that touch.

Actually, Todd, I'm certain that everyone who's ever gone toe-to-toe with you wishes your hands were as soft as Selanne's, and not for just five minutes. They'd undoubtedly be wearing a whole lot less scar tissue.

# Rubber Gems

## Using Your Head to Get an Official Game Puck

Every culture has its medium of exchange, a system whereby certain items represent a set value and can be exchanged for desired goods and services. Primitive cultures traded in beads or furs, while modern societies have created complicated forms of legal tender, such as bills and coinage. In the world of hockey souvenirs, the legal tender is the Puck. Costing almost nothing to manufacture, pucks nevertheless have a significant collector market value. And because the replacement game pucks are kept in the penalty box, I'm the one who stands between collectors and their prize.

Just as with money, different kinds of pucks have different values. Souvenir pucks are any of a variety of pucks which have a team logo, player picture, or advertisement printed on them, but are not actually used in a National Hockey League game. These pucks are readily available at hockey shops and arenas, and can be purchased relatively inexpensively. They are fun for the kids and make cute little conversation pieces.

Then there are the Official National Hockey League Game Pu These are for the big kids.

In the world of hockey souvenirs, the legal tender is the Puck.

Looking much like souvenir pucks, the Official National Hockey League Game Puck has distinctive imprints on both sides, much like a twenty-dollar double eagle gold coin. On the front side is the team logo in authentic color and detail. On the back side, or obverse as the collectors say, is the traditional orange imprint stating "Official Game Puck," and carrying the carefully reproduced signature of NHL Commissioner Gary Bettman. The desirability of these pucks is quite high, because obtaining one is very rare, usually only after it's just bounced off the head of the fan sitting next to you.

Although warned at the start of every National Hockey League game that the puck may at any time turn into a heat-seeking missile, fans are nevertheless injured when they decide to read the program during game time. This while sitting above glass level in a seat behind one of the nets. Bad move. Worst move? Some fans, high in courage but low in their understanding of physics, intentionally put themselves in harm's way hoping they can grab the puck just before they lapse into unconsciousness.

One attractive young lady sitting in a well-known puck landing area was in the process of eating, and faster than you can say "incoming," she was hit by an errant shot. Drenched in blood, she jumped screaming from her seat. Even the players stopped skating to stare at this horribly injured fan. It wasn't until the usher reached her with a first-aid kit that it was discovered the puck actually landed in her plate of french fries, and she was covered not in blood, but in ketchup. Her screams were probably because didn't even end up with the puck. That went to the guy sitting in the behind her.

s were going to great lengths to try and get one of these rubber gems, some even offering a lot of cold, hard cash for just one cold, hard puck. When told they cannot be sold or given away, things usually got nasty. Getting around the arena without being aggressively panhandled for a puck was impossible to do. Then a miracle happened.

For the 1995–96 season, someone had the bright idea to make all game pucks generic by removing the team logo, and replacing it with the NHL logo on both sides. This, of course, made all pucks appear the same. Puck begging dropped to almost nothing. I could once again stroll the arena openly and without fear of attack from puck-hungry hordes.

But someone clearly unconcerned about my personal safety reinstituted the team logo pucks for the 1996–97 season. Now everything's just the

*Nothing is more collectible than an official NHL puck, and some fans will do just a* *anything to get their hands on one.*

way it used to be. It's so depressing having to go back to avoiding collectors in a rubber feeding frenzy by sneaking around the Pond.

But it's had the opposite effect on the fans. They're once again happi-
ly putting their heads in the way of flying pucks.

# The Grate Comeback

## Defensive Play in the Penalty Box

With the second selection in the 1987 entry draft, New Jersey had a tough decision to make. Buffalo had already chosen high-scoring Pierre Turgeon from the Quebec Major Junior Hockey League. Still available to the Devils was an even higher scorer in Joe Sakic, who was filling the net for the Swift Current Broncos. Having finished the season out of the playoffs for the ninth consecutive season, New Jersey desperately needed the soft hands of a natural scorer, and Sakic's 130 points proved he had those.

But they needed something else that was just as important. Tired of being kicked around in their own division, they needed a big forward who could score knockouts as well as goals. Somebody who would show up, not just in the slot, but in the corners as well. Of concern to the deci-sion-makers in East Rutherford were Sakic's other numbers: just 5' 11", 185 pounds, and only 31 PIM.

The Devils' attention began to shift elsewhere, and eventually focused on the Ontario Hockey League, where a local boy from Mimico wa putting up impressive numbers on both sides of the ledger for Lond Not only were Brendan Shanahan's numbers a perfect match that sea 92 points and 92 penalty minutes, he looked like a perfect match f rigors of the National Hockey League at 6' 3" and 218 pounds. As an added bonus best understood by management and groupies, his rugged, movie star looks would undoubtedly help boost the declining box office.

Picking Shanny paid immediate dividends for the Devils. In the following season, they beat the Islanders and the Capitals before they lost the conference championship to Boston in seven games. And while he didn't win the Calder Trophy, Brendan's totals for production (29 points) and protection (175 penalty minutes) made him an important part of the Devil's new-found success.

These numbers would steadily rise to a career high in the 1993–94 season of 109 points and 215 penalty minutes, making Shanahan the prototypical power forward, a force to be reckoned with whether he's carrying the puck or dropping the gloves.

By contrast, Jason York almost sneaked out of the Ontario Hockey League, Detroit taking him 129th overall in the 1990 entry draft. Not only chosen way behind solid defensemen Darryl Sydor and Derian Hatcher, York was taken behind Etienne Belzile and Terran Sandwith as well. What the Red Wings saw, however, was a good-sized defenseman at 6' 2" and a shade under 200 pounds, who played with a discipline that usually kept him out of the penalty box and in play. In his last season with the Windsor Spitfires, he contributed 80 helpers for 93 total points, while spending less than half that time in the sin bin. Jason had developed a willpower of steel to minimize reacting to cheapshots and wisecracks that would leave his team on the short end of the stick.

## PENALTY BOX

**Brendan Shanahan**
Games Played: 879
Total Points: 814
Penalty Minutes: 1,187

Traded to the Mighty Ducks of Anaheim for the 1995–96 season, Jason York would have that willpower put to the test, first in the slot, then in the box, with Hartford's newly

*Almost never at a loss for words, Brendan Shanahan was struck dumb by a Jas* insult.

acquired captain, Brendan Shanahan.

During a late season game pitting the two cross-continent rivals, Shanahan seemed intent on practicing the late Coach Fred Shero's philosophy: to arrive at the net in ill spirits. Shoving his way into the slot for a screen test with Guy Hebert, Shanny came shoulder to shoulder with York, neither one willing to yield that single square foot of ice that could make the difference between a tip-in or a glove save. When push came to shove, the whistle blew signaling a trip for two to the penalty box.

Once in the box, York calmly took his seat, but Shanny was in high gear. Literally standing over me, he kept up a continuous verbal assault on York, who just kept staring out onto the ice as if he didn't hear a word.

"When I get outta here, I'm gonna tear you up. I'm gonna hurt you big time. You're gonna regret it. They'll be carryin' you outta here when I'm done with you."

On and on it went as York continued to silently stare out at the play on the ice. The Off-Ice Officials looked back and forth from Shanahan to York expecting the vehement comeback that never came. Suddenly, a big cheer went up from the crowd signaling a Ducks' score. At that, Shanahan went wild. Eyes bulging, he stepped up his haranguing, hurling insult after insult at the stoic York.

"That ices it. As soon as I'm out, I'm gonna butt end you in the face. They better have a doctor ready cause . . . "

Just then, York slowly turned, looked directly at Shanahan, and completely without expression said in an even voice: "Why don't you just shut up, you toothless #@%$^&".

Completely stunned, Brendan's mouth dropped open. The expression

## PENALTY BOX

**Jason York**
Games Played: 275
Total Points: 77
Penalty Minutes: 244

on his face was one of complete shock as he stared in disbelief at York, who had once again turned all his attention back to the ice. Stammering, Shanahan kept repeating over and over, "T-toothless. He called me toothless," as if checking to see if he had really heard

> Brendan seemed taken aback that anyone would have the nerve to insult his looks.

it right. Having been routinely picked by the media as the best-looking player in the National Hockey League, Brendan seemed taken aback that anyone would have the nerve to insult his looks.

It was obvious to all that the next step was for Shanahan to try to use his stick either as a javelin or a pitchfork, so everyone started looking for cover. Much to our surprise, Shanahan simply stopped talking, and took a seat on the penalty box bench. Concerned he was merely conserving his energy for a more direct response to Jason, I signaled the linesmen to be ready for Brendan's release. With everyone on full alert, both players stepped out of their boxes, and without so much as a glance at each other, skated directly to their respective benches. Amazingly, although Shanahan and York were on the ice together several shifts during the rest of the game, the promised retaliation never came.

Brendan Shanahan's numbers, both in points and penalties, prove he plays at an extreme intensity level. By contrast, Jason York is a man of few words who lets his play do his talking for him. But obviously, when he does speak, he has the knack for saying just enough.

# What *Not* to Say to Mario!

## A Lost Invitation to Fan Appreciation Night

It was only four-thirty in the afternoon, and yet the entire Off-Ice Officials Crew was already at the rink. They weren't the only ones early, either. Over a thousand fans were already queuing up at the doors, which wouldn't open for another ninety minutes. Even if you didn't know the schedule, you could tell something special was on tap.

The Mighty Ducks would be facing off against the Pittsburgh Penguins in their only stop at the Arrowhead Pond for the 1996–97 season. More importantly, this might be the last time local fans would be able to see Mario Lemieux play professional hockey. For some time, unconfirmed reports had been circulating throughout the league that Mario the Magnifique would retire at the end of the season.

Not since Bobby Orr began his professional career in 1966 had a player entered the National Hockey League to such acclaim. His last year in junior hockey was a hint of offense to come. In 70 games for Laval of the Quebec Major Junior Hockey League, Lemieux scored an astounding 282 points. Not only did he have the moves, he was big. Real big. At 6' 4" and 225 pounds, he could skate through traffic as if he had a police esco* Trying to stop him was enough to put defensemen in sanitariums. Wit*

> Anytime you can get Mario Lemieux off the ice, even if only for two minutes, it's well worth it.

reach that put the puck out front, and a long stride to keep it there, every trip to the net was a candidate for a highlight film.

In his all-too-brief career, Mario Lemieux would win six Art Ross Trophies as the league's leading scorer. Not bad for a guy who never played a complete season in the National Hockey League. The debate will undoubtedly wage eternal as to which of the two great players was the best of his time, if not all time: Wayne or Mario. But on this night the house was packed with those who wanted to see a contest between the man in the lead for yet another scoring title, and the youngster who was trying to catch him, Paul Kariya.

Frustrated by their inability to stop this scoring machine, other teams had perfected a two-step approach to keeping Mario off the scoreboard: 1) clutch, and 2) grab. It became apparent that on this night, the Mighty Ducks would use the same two steps in the hopes they could pick up two points. To be successful, this technique is employed when the player being stalked does not have possession of the puck. Despite the bright arena lighting, Mario would have one, sometimes two shadows intent on keeping themselves between him and the action for the entirety of the game. Frustrated by a style of play he regarded as detrimental to the sport of hockey, he began to take matters into his own hands.

In the first period, Mario took a two minute minor obviously designed to send a message to his shadow: keep your distance. But with him getting the penalty, it only seemed to intensify the rough stuff. Anytime you can get Mario Lemieux off the ice, even if only for two minutes, it's well worth it.

Sitting next to him in the penalty box reminded me of one other time

*An ill-considered comment by a Ducks fan sent the always dangerous Mario Lemieux on a scoring tear.*

**Mario Lemieux**
Games Played: 834
Total Points: 1,649
**Penalty Minutes:** 820

I had been that close to the Big Man. Several years before, he was in Los Angeles being treated for his back problems, and had attended the Penguins-Kings game as a spectator. A friend of his agent was kind enough to set up a meeting in the Forum parking lot between Mario and my son and I, where he graciously signed my son's hockey jersey, card, and baseball cap. I wanted to thank him again for his kindness to my son, but it would have been inappropriate to do so. He was getting pestered enough out on the ice without having to deal with it in the box as well.

Near the start of the second period, Mario once again picked up a minor, much to the satisfaction of the home crowd. He was making a statement, all right, but it was being lost in the Penalty Timekeeper's notes.

By the middle of the second period, Lemieux had no goals, but had just been assessed his third minor penalty. For that, he received a roar from the crowd that only served to irritate him more than the call itself. As he made his way into the box, the look on his face showed clearly the kind of night he was having. But thanks to an anonymous voice in the crowd, all that was to change, and quickly.

Just as the crowd noise had died down, a loudmouth fan sitting near the penalty box yelled out, "Hey, big shot. You just got a hat trick in penalties."

Mario acted as if he never heard it, but the flinch when it was said suggested he had heard the same thing we had. Nothing was said, but Mario was up with 30 seconds left in the penalty waiting for the door to open. It seemed then that he had some point he wanted to make.

The Penguins suddenly caught fire after that penalty, spanking the

Mighty Ducks 7–3. Sadly, Mario did call it quits that season, and he did so with 39 career hat tricks. And if you look in the record books, you'll find that one of them was scored that night, December 11, 1996. What you won't see is an assist to some wise guy in the stands.

# Between Periods

## (Not in the Highlight Reels)

Something truly amazing happens between the periods of a hockey game. No, it's not the entertainment, which ranges from ice dancing and acrobatics to mini-mite games. And it's not the replays of big hits or top ten goals shown on the Jumbotron. To someone like me who grew up playing hockey in the forties and fifties, it's watching the Zambonis resurface the ice.

What now takes a matter of only a few minutes was once a drawn-out affair requiring the activity of nearly a dozen able-bodied men who would emerge from behind the boards in a swarm, each carrying tools which have long since become relics of a bygone era. Dressed in brightly-colored jackets identifying them as members of the prestigious Ice Crew, they would set about performing their assigned tasks in an almost ritual-like manner.

The first man out would scramble along the base of the boards furiously jabbing at the ice with a six-inch wide long-handled scraper. Ice chips would fly everywhere as he worked his way around the perimeter of the rink. Right on his heels would be the sweeper, who would use a large broom to sweep those same ice chips away from the edge of the rink.

The crowd would cheer as they scurried around the rink in near-perfect synch.

Once the board scraper and sweeper were done, the large scraper team would assemble at one end of the rink. Four guys each holding a three-foot wide steel-bladed scraper would stand shoulder to shoulder with their blades slightly overlapping one another. In lock step, they would proceed to walk around the rink in decreasing circles stopping near the entrance at the end of each lap to deposit the accumulated snow in what would ultimately become a miniature Matterhorn. Around and around they would walk until the rink had been thoroughly scraped clean of snow and ice chips. Then the entire crew would attack the mountain of snow, shovelling it into a caravan of wheelbarrows for transportation to some secret place. For years we were certain it became the main ingredient for the snow cones sold rinkside.

The grand finale began when the last man would walk through the rink gate dragging the longest hose imaginable, and go to the farthest corner where he would begin spraying a fine mist of water. Skillfully avoiding the chain link fence that was the forerunner of tempered glass, and the fans seated beyond, he would coat the entire surface with water as he backed in a serpentine pattern across and eventually out of the rink. Magically the water would slowly turn into a perfect sheet of ice right before our very eyes. Total elapsed time: about 25 minutes.

Of course, what we didn't know, and Frank J. Zamboni did, was that it was far from a perfect sheet of ice. Manual scraping merely removed the surface snow, leaving behind ruts and holes. Because the water could not be applied uniformly, pools were frozen into an uneven, rippled texture that would cause the puck to hop and skip as if it had a will of its own.

Plus, it took the equivalent of a period of play to make it. Time to get a hot dog? Fans had almost enough time to go home and cook a meal.

Something had to be done, and Frank was just the guy to do it.

Starting in 1939, Zamboni spent ten years creating a working model of a self-propelled machine that would uniformly sweep, scrape, and resurface a rink. Effective it was, pretty it wasn't. It had all the grace of a tractor. Gradually refining the original design of the 1949 Model A, Zamboni sales began to take off. Eventually, one was purchased for use in the St. Paul Auditorium, home of the St. Paul Fighting Saints Professional Hockey Club.

Rumor had it that such a contraption existed, and that it would make its debut at the upcoming game between the Minneapolis Millers and the Fighting Saints. Anticipation was high as the first period ended. Several of the players stayed behind to watch history in the making. As the end

*Sparking a revolution in ice resurfacing, the Zamboni brought the days of the prestigious Ice Crew to an end.*

> **Anticipation was high as the first period ended. Several of the players stayed behind to watch history in the making.**

boards were opened, a loud engine could be heard sparking to life. After several moments of suspense, a large, oblong form appeared, sputtering noisily as it made its way onto and around the ice.

The crowd was eerily silent, staring in disbelief as the machine single-handedly resurfaced the ice. I could see the ice crew staring through the chain link watching the machine ice the rink and their celebrity. Each had the mournful look of assembly line workers at a GM plant closing. As it finished its last pass down the ice, a cheer started, slowly at first, then reaching a deafening crescendo of applause, whistles, and foot-stomping.

From that night on, the "Zam" was the biggest draw at the game. Kids wanted to sit on it and have their picture taken with it. Parents wanted to know how it worked. Farmers wanted to know if it could also bale hay.

Each time I watch the ice being resurfaced, I think back to that first night I saw the Zamboni perform its own ice show, and the excitement of the crowd at seeing ice and history in the making. Unfortunately the rise of the Zamboni signaled the end for the Ice Crew, their time in the spotlight over. Not seeing them at the games anymore, I asked my dad what had become of them. I remember being greatly consoled when he told me that he had heard that each was hired full-time at the Ford Motor Company plant right there in St. Paul. And talk about good fortune—they were going to be working on Ford's all-new car of the future, the Edsel. Some people have all the luck.

# Speak to Us

## A Front Row Seat at the Soapbox

Before, after, and sometimes even during the game, players are besieged by the media in hopes that a press conference, interview or even casual conversation will produce that memorable quote that makes the next day's headline. More often than not, what is said is less memorable than forgettable. Prodding the player usually results in something unprintable. Baiting a player could be suicidal. But for many players, the penalty box becomes their soapbox. Realizing that getting the last word may be more devastating than landing the last punch, each becomes a veritable orator—Pericles with a mouthpiece. Through broken noses and missing teeth comes the wit and wisdom of hockey, some of which is recorded in the following events.

*****

Ronnie Stern of the Calgary Flames is no stranger to the penalty box. When healthy, and in a good mood, he can rack up more than 200 penalty minutes in a season. If really pressed, as he apparently was in the 1991–92 season, he can to get over 300 minutes in penalties. Obviously, he's had every penalty in the book called on him at some point in his nine-year National Hockey League career. But he heard one he'd never heard

## Through broken noses and missing teeth comes the wit and wisdom of hockey.

before during one game against the Ducks.

As Stern sat on the bench between shifts, a fight broke out right in front of him between one of the Ducks and one of the Calgary strongmen, Paul Kruse. Not content with having a ringside seat, Ronnie stood, and at times leaned over the boards yelling encouragement to Cruiser.

Soon enough, the battle was over and the two combatants were shown to their respective penalty boxes. But as the referee called off the penalties, he also gave Ronnie two minutes. When a shocked Stern asked what his penalty was, someone yelled out, "You got two minutes for looking, Stern."

*****

After receiving a penalty by one of the shortest referees in the National Hockey League, the particularly large player argued his case, but to no avail. As the referee skated away, the player yelled after him,

"You're nothing but a nine iron!"

*****

Bad Boy Bob Probert came in the penalty box to serve two minutes on a penalty he felt he didn't deserve. As Bob took his seat, I closed the penalty box door, and sat down next to him. Seeing the Referee skate by the box, Probert suddenly leaped up and pulled open the door.

"That was a @^$#&* call," slammed it shut, and sat back down.

After the game, my supervisor came up to me, and having seen the incident with Probie, said, "Don't let them open the door like that!"

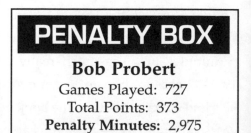

**PENALTY BOX**

**Bob Probert**
Games Played: 727
Total Points: 373
**Penalty Minutes:** 2,975

*Shayne Corson knows how to handle both defenders on the ice and hecklers in the stands.*

**PENALTY BOX**

**Ronnie Stern**
Games Played: 527
Total Points: 149
**Penalty Minutes:** 1,870

Yeah, sure. Me and what army?

\*\*\*\*\*

Shayne Corson has played with distinction on a number of National Hockey League teams. On two of them, the Montreal Canadiens and the Edmonton Oilers, he was selected as team captain. It was common knowledge that Corson was being paid handsomely for both his leadership and hockey skill.

During a game between the Mighty Ducks and the Oilers, Corson was escorted to the penalty box to spend a little quiet time after an altercation with a Duck defenseman. As he took his seat, a fan sitting close to the penalty box yelled,

"Hey, Corson, who's stupid enough to pay you all that money?"

Corson turned and looked at the heckler, and with a deadpan expression answered:

"Well, I guess you are, seeing as how you paid to get in here tonight."

\*\*\*\*\*

After scoring a one-sided victory in a scrap with a Mighty Ducks forward, a player took his seat in the visitors' penalty box. A particularly heavy, dare I say obese, Ducks fan was standing nearby and loudly cheering the referee's call. The player simply glanced in the fan's direction, and in a chilling tone yelled,

"Sit down, Fatso!"

Whether out of fear or simply an admission to being overweight, everyone within earshot, including me, immediately sat down.

\*\*\*\*\*

Some fans have commented in the past about what a great seat the goal judge has for watching the game. In fact, you don't get to watch the game, only the puck. And sometimes that's a lot harder to do than you might think.

**PENALTY BOX**

**Shayne Corson**
Games Played: 912
Total Points: 585
**Penalty Minutes:** 1,938

In one home game, the Ducks were on a power play, and in classic style were clogging the front of the net hoping to screen the goalie. As the puck was passed by one defenseman along the blue line to his partner, I turned just as he one-timed a rocket that I didn't see until it was about two feet in front of me and coming right at my head.

Reflexively, I did what any terrified person would do, I ducked. The impact of the puck on the glass was so loud that I thought my ears were ringing. It took almost a minute for me to realize that it was actually the telephone in my box that was ringing. Straightening back up, I picked up the phone just in time to hear the crew supervisor say,

"Great! I've got a goal judge who ducks when the puck is shot."

# Kicking the Bucket

## Bringing the Fight Off the Ice and Into the Penalty Box

The most difficult job for a referee is not spotting a penalty, but calling it. The penalty in most cases is so obvious, people listening to the game on the radio can even spot it. The reason it's difficult to call is that the referee knows once his arm goes up, he's often in for Oscar-winning snivelling.

Some players are fairly subtle about it. A slow shaking of the head coupled with a hang dog look is their most aggressive form of pleading. Others step it up a notch by verbalizing their defense, complete with appropriate hand gestures and facial expressions. A cross between F. Lee Bailey and F. Murray Abraham, their act could play on Broadway. Ultimately, they accept their fate, but can still be seen wildly gesturing even as the penalty box door closes on them.

Then there are the extremists. These are people who use every means possible to plead not only their own cases, but those of oppressed peoples everywhere. And their histrionics don't stop once they reach the box. In fact, this is where it can, and often does, reach its crescendo. Hurling water bottles, tape rolls, and towels to underscore the injustice, they usually succeed in working a two minute minor into a ten minute misconduct while destroying the penalty box. During my tour of duty, I've seen several players fall

**The Penalty Time Record began to read like the Table of Contents of the NHL Rule Book.**

into this category, taking out their anger and frustrations not on the referee or other players, but on the defenseless penalty box itself. In one memorable moment, however, I saw the box strike back, and exact revenge for penalty boxes everywhere.

During the later part of the 1994–95 season the Mighty Ducks were set to play the San Jose Sharks, a divisional rival bent on proving their National Hockey League superiority. Predictions before the game were that this would be a penalty-filled contest, and no sooner had the first puck been dropped than everyone knew the predictions were going to become reality.

Interference, hooking, tripping. The Penalty Time Record began to read like the Table of Contents of the NHL Rule Book. Goalie interference. Holding the stick. On it went. One after another, players from both sides streamed in and out of the penalty boxes. Crowd noise was barely audible over the steady shriek of the referee's whistle. Penalty boxes filled as it began to seem the real contest was which team would get the most penalties, not the most goals.

With two players already in my penalty box, the referee's whistle blew yet again as he signaled another penalty to the visiting team. As the player, who for his own protection and ego shall remain nameless, headed towards the box, it became clear he was not the shy and retiring type. After the linesmen literally shoved him into the box and skated away, it dawned on him that his appeal had not only been denied, but ignored. Now even more infuriated, he glanced around the already crowded box for something to vent his frustrations on. It was then that he spied the puck bucket sitting almost at his feet.

Containing approximately two dozen pucks in a bed of crushed ice, the rather innocent looking white bucket stands 19" high and is 13" in diameter, and weighs in at a trim 4 lbs, 3 oz. Thinking this would be the harmless foil for a tantrum, he drew his leg back and kicked the side of the bucket as hard as he could. So hard that his skate blade penetrated through the plastic bucket, sending a spray of ice and water into the air. Surprised by the unexpected water show, he attempted to subtly pull his skate loose only to find that it had clamped firmly into the bucket's side. It should be noted that this bucket is made of polyethylene vinyl, a space-age, lightweight plastic polymer known for its extreme strength and durability. And as was about to be demonstrated, its amazing staying power.

Awkwardly trying to get his skate free, he violently shook it, but the

*The Mighty Ducks and San Jose Sharks square off for California bragging rights, resulting in a penalty-filled game.*

bucket held fast, like a Gila monster. Continuing to yank and pull as hard as he could, the player could not unlock the bucket's vice-like grip. In frustration compounded by humiliation, he made one last mighty shake which only caused the bucket to erupt like a frozen Mt. Vesuvius. Ice chips, water, and even pucks flew through the air. The others in the box began yelling for him to stop.

"We shower after the game, not during it."

"You're gonna drown us all."

Having mercy on him, as well as a good laugh, one of his teammates finally helped free him from the bucket's clutches.

When his penalty expired and he left the box, the floor was littered with remnants of this epic battle. I had to wonder how he must have felt after being bested by the most unlikely adversary. It's one thing to lose to Dave Manson or Craig Berube, but losing to Tupperware has to be hard to handle.

# Index

## Photo Credits